# She Changed Me *one ordeal, two perspectives*

# Mike Chisholm

# She Changed Me

*One Ordeal, Two Perspectives*

# Mike Chisholm

*LIGHTBRINGER | PODCASTER | GRANDFATHER*

*DON'T FOCUS ON THE PROBLEM:*
*FOCUS ON THE SOLUTION*

Daring to Share Global

Published by Mike and Candace Chisholm
September 2021 ISBN: 9781777939205

Editor: Diana Reyers
Typeset: Greg Salisbury
Book Cover Design: Kodie Beckley & Elara Isagawa

*For Elara*

# Testimonial

*I met Mike through our work in the community a few years ago. Our first meeting was initially planned to be short and to the point. However, once we finished our official business of the day, we started a great conversation about our music, where we live, and our families.*

*George Michael music was, of course, part of the conversation since Mike and I are around the same age. We both love Kelowna, so we chatted a lot about how blessed we are to live there. Then, we started a very long conversation about his new granddaughter, Elara, and he proudly showed me many photos of her on his cellphone. I am sure she takes up all the storage on his phone! She is beautiful, smiling in every photo with her eyes lit up from the attention she is receiving! Her beautiful curly hair immediately caught my attention! Mike was already madly in love with that little lady.*

*With his heart full, he mentioned how she brought so much joy to his family. I had never seen such a proud Grandpa. As we chatted more, we realized I had met his wife, Candace, at a women's networking event a few months before. I recalled that she was as friendly and welcoming as Mike. What a great opportunity to meet this incredible couple who brighten our community every day.*

*After meeting him, I started following Mike and Candace on social media more often. They are funny and kind, with many qualities that are important to me in relationships. Their dedication to family and friends is to be commended. They are a genuine couple and so inspirational to others.*

*I was fortunate to be invited to one of Candace's Birthday parties and got to see how others clearly felt the same about this happy, enthusiastic woman! Of course, Mike was at her side the whole time, which shows the brilliance of this couple.*

*When Mike and Candace announced the journey they were about to go through with Elara, my heart sank for them. But I also knew that their dedication as Grandparents would help her get through her treatments. This book is a testament to what deep love, focused time, dedication, and patience can accomplish when moving through good or bad times.*

*Even though the brilliant title, "She Changed Me" is how Mike and Candace feel about Elara, I believe as community, we are also experiencing how Elara changed us. We were invited into a very private part of them, rooting for a family who deserved to continue living the life they had planned.*

*Watching Elara grow brings me joy, especially when she's looking at the camera with her big smile and bright eyes. She is so loved by her community, and she doesn't even know it yet!*

Sarah Shakespeare
sarahshakespeare.com

# Foreword

## By Gloria Cuccione

I am honoured to write the foreword for this book because I understand too well from personal experience what is required to struggle through the depths of fear and despair and come out the other side stronger, hopeful, and even optimistic. This is a story of one little girl's journey and survival through the nightmare of childhood cancer shared through the eyes of both her grandparents. Elara's story is one of tragedy turned to triumph.

I believe that I was destined to meet Mike and Candy, Elara's grandparents, and the authors of this book. The connection we felt because of the similar journey we experienced was undeniable. I am so proud of them for staying close and not allowing this disease to destroy the love and support they have for one other. I know that it has been a rough road with many pitfalls along the way and times when they felt alone. I am awed by their strength and depth of love for each other and how they drew hope from every success along the way—big or small. Elara led the way on this journey with a unique innocence, joy and hope that only a child can bring.

I will never forget the devastation when our son Michael was diagnosed with Hodgkin's lymphoma at age nine. Our world was turned upside down—never to be the same again! With a bone marrow transplant and chemotherapy, Michael won his battle with cancer but sadly passed away at the age of 16 due to respiratory complications. We have been asked many times, "How can you be so strong?" The answer is surprisingly simple. When you have a child that navigates this ordeal always with a smile on his face and a positive attitude, how can you not stay strong?

My son, Michael Cuccione, imagined a world without childhood cancer and pledged to 'Make a Difference' in the fight against this disease. At the beginning of his diagnosis, he started writing his own songs and put a CD out raising $130,000. When asked what he wanted to do with this money, his response was, "I want to fund young researchers and find the cure for childhood cancer". Although he accomplished much in his short life, the Michael Cuccione Foundation (MCF) that he founded in 1997 to raise awareness and funding for childhood cancer research remains his greatest achievement. Michael's family and friends continue his legacy through the MCF, raising in excess of $25M to support research at the Michael Cuccione Childhood Cancer Research Program (MCCCRP) at BC Children's Hospital.

Researchers at the MCCCRP at BC Children's Hospital continue to break new ground in understanding and treating paediatric cancer. With every step taken, this research translates into innovative and life-saving therapies and improvements in the overall health and quality of life for children and young adults living with cancer around the world. In 2019, the MCF was instrumental in bringing CAR-T cell therapy to BC by helping fund BC Children's Hospital participation in CureWorks, an international collaboration of leading academic pediatric hospitals around the world, focusing on improving care for children with hard-to-treat cancers. Today, there are children in BC thriving thanks to this life-saving treatment, without which they would have been sent home with no hope. This immunotherapy has shown great promise for children with certain types of relapsed leukaemia, lymphoma and other blood cancers. More research is needed for solid tumours, so the MCF is now looking to the future and taking steps to fund the next step in CAR-T cell therapy. Please visit www.childhoodcancerresearch.org for more information.

Michael had a vision and believed that "One person can only do so much, but together we can make a difference!" We will find a cure and give hope to all the children like Elara that are touched by childhood cancer.

This book is about an honest and heart-wrenching journey that changes your life forever—with all the ups and downs, twists and turns that come with the diagnosis of cancer in a young child. It is also a message of insights, survival, hope and winning the battle without losing each other. I know this book will help so many people navigate through the challenge.

**We will continue to keep Elara and her family in our thoughts and prayers!**

**Gloria Cuccione**

Gloria Cuccione is the mother of the late Michael Cuccione, Founder, and inspiration behind the Michael Cuccione Foundation. Gloria has been the driving force, continuing Michael's legacy and vision through his Foundation. Gloria is the recipient of the Order of British Columbia awarded in 2014 as well as the Queen Elizabeth II Diamond Jubilee Award in 2012.

# Introduction

## By Candace Chisholm

Every couple with differing opinions, despite going through the same trial, needs to read this book. It is different from most, if not any, book you have read before. The flip over, upside down, read from the back to the middle, is much more than just a clever gimmick—it's about perspective, diversity, and acceptance. This book takes the same situation and sees it through two completely lenses. It humanizes what a challenging experience can and will do to you, and makes allowances for the way you'll react, which can be totally opposite to what you would expect. This book will make you cry, wince, laugh, and exhale, sometimes all at the same time.

And here is a secret. I only read Mike's side of the story *AFTER* I completed mine. That's right. You read that correctly. We wrote our entire manuscripts apart from each other, never once asking the other what they were putting down on this magic paper. Our wonderful editor, Diana, was the only one who read each of our chapters as they came in. We had trust in our story, we had trust in her, and most of all, we had trust each other. So, what did I think....?

I never doubted the impact his words would make, but I was unprepared for the reverberation they continually have on me. Mike's book is like walking out onto the observation deck of his soul. Each word peels back the skin of his deepest feelings, and I felt all of them with him. He throws the traditional man-up ideology out the door and brazenly shows you his fears, his shortcomings, but most importantly, his unyielding love. You will read about gratitude in such an open and honest way, it will make you blush. And, you will have a front row seat to his devotion to a little girl, who actually **changed him**.

I am proud to have written this with Mike, and I am grateful to have a partner who loves so purely. I am excited for you to know him. He's my oak tree—strong and rooted, providing life-saving oxygen when needed. I have known for some time who this man is...and now you will too. It's a gift.

With love

Candy
September 2021

# She Changed Me

# I

# Instinct

On December 22nd, 2019, I experienced one of the greatest moments of my entire life. Outside, it was a beautiful winter wonderland, and my wife and I were hosting our then 20-month-old granddaughter, Elara, at our house for the night. Ever since Elara was born, we made it a habit to have her sleep over as much as possible. We are over the moon in love with this little person. Not only is she an absolutely adorable child, but she has this certain *something* about her. It's hard to describe because I am sure most grandparents feel the same way about their offspring's offspring. But this little one is different, and I understand most grandparents say that too!

That being said, I still maintain Elara is somehow different. From the day she was born, complete strangers would randomly approach us when they saw us hanging out with Elara. They would just want to tell us how beautiful she is and how they are drawn to her for some inexplicable reason. Many would tell us she's an old soul. My wife, Candy, and I are young grandparents, so many people think Elara is our daughter when they see us with her, and I rarely correct them because I'm so proud of the kid. She is a gorgeous gift from somewhere beyond this earth, and I treasure her more than my or nearly any other life.

Going back to the night of December 22nd, Candy and I thought it would be a great idea to bundle her up and take her to see the holiday lights and decorations. We just had a snowfall with the biggest fluffy flakes, and it wasn't too cold—the perfect winter night. We heard there was a block party in our neighbourhood, and a lot of houses were decked out in enough holiday cheer to keep the electric company happy for years. Elara looked adorable as usual in her toque and white faux fur coat that Candy purchased for her. One of the little pleasures we get in our lives is the kick we get out of dressing that kid.

As we walked by each illuminated house, quite a few people stopped to take in the reaction of excitement and wonder on Elara's face. It was magical. At the centre of it all, one neighbour had a band playing music in their carport—older stuff like Van Morrison and the Beatles—and they provided hot chocolate and goodies in the front yard. It was a wonderful neighbourhood gathering with hundreds of people celebrating on that snowy suburban street.

I have no idea what the band's name was, but it was the catalyst for the ethereal moment I experienced. Elara heard the music and went running towards it with the reckless abandon of a one-year-old. Running between the happy neighbours, she made her way to the front of the crowd to stand right in front of the band, and she began to dance. Candy and I stood on the side beaming with pride as our tiny granddaughter instantly became the centre of attention. Mid song, the band focused on her and actually began playing for her like she was their audience of one. Everyone laughed when Elara clapped or swayed and bopped to the music. She often let out a loud exclamation of glee. Our granddaughter was in her element, enjoying every moment of it.

The band asked us what her name was and then suddenly changed the lyrics to some 70s song to include *Elara* while serenading her. But cute as that was, it isn't the magical moment

I am referring to. That moment presented itself when the band began playing *Runaway* by Del Shannon. Elara started dancing again. I squatted down, she came over, and we started dancing together. I spun her around in that *awkward-dancing-with-a-cute-baby* kinda way, and she melted into me and gave me a kiss.

**Now, I'm a pretty sensitive guy at the best of times, and she captured my heart the day she was born, so that little move made me tear up a bit.**

She continued to dance for the band, and the neighbours continued to look on. I turned to my wife and told her: *This is one of the greatest moments of my life.* It was then that I realized Candy had the ol' telephone out and was capturing the whole thing on video. I do realize it wasn't me the video was committed to. Candy loves Elara more than I do, but hey, I am happy to be the costar to the main attraction in these home movies. I probably watched that video 50 times after our baby angel went to bed that night, and every time, emotion rose from within. I remember that night because Candace and I took the opportunity to map out the rest of the holiday season while talking about my business plan for the new year. We also discussed a trip we had coming up; just she and I were getting away to Disneyland right after New Year's. That night, I actually wrote down how grateful I was in a journal I keep; I thought life could not get any better.

Three days later, we were in the paediatric wing of our local general hospital, where a very nice doctor, along with an equally nice, registered nurse, sat down with us and Elara's parents, our son and daughter-in-law. They let us know that Elara had a mass the size of an orange just behind her tail bone, and we needed to go to BC Children's Hospital in Vancouver as a next step. As it turns out, the night after our whimsical winter evening, Candy noticed a little bump just above Elara's adorable little bum crack while taking her out of the bath. We instantly recalled that Elara had a really hard time filling her diaper that morning, and not for lack of trying. She was constipated, and we were helpless as she tried to push out her situation. This was a massive poo that wanted out. She actually screamed while passing it, and it looked a little different than her past fecal leavings. *It looked older* —if that makes sense— like it had been in there longer than it should have been. Candy thought perhaps our gorgeous granddaughter could have some impacted poo or something, and it might be wise to take her in and get it checked.

When the kids arrived to collect their daughter, Candy told them about the lump. We were intentionally gentle in the delivery because Candy's son, my stepson, and his wife were new parents. We didn't want to worry them, but we did want to convey the sense of urgency we felt. As new grandparents, we constantly walk the line of being more relaxed than the new mommy and daddy. Within that, we still want to be respectful of their wishes while spoiling the hell out of Elara. If we didn't balance that all out, we would spoil the kid all the time as a full-time job! Candy successfully communicated what was going on, and she accompanied them to the hospital that night. Elara got an ultrasound, and we didn't think much about them wanting to give her another one the next day when the daytime staff was on shift. They wanted to be thorough; to look at things more conclusively was what we told ourselves. However, we did raise our eyebrows when asked to return for an MRI the day after that. Three days in a row to the hospital? Hmmmm. That did set off a bit of a red flag because, normally, it can be tricky to get an MRI in a timely fashion for those of us who live in

Canada. We know this because of personal experience; in 2015, my wife was given a three to five month wait time to have an MRI to see if she had MS—thank goodness she doesn't. But the fact they had an MRI lined up for Elara that quickly and on Christmas Eve no less was something that definitely got our attention. We chalked it up to the fact that they gave Elara priority because she was so young, and we hoped for the best.

That morning was the first time I felt traumatized seeing a child receiving medical treatment. It certainly wasn't the last time, but oh boy, I will never forget the first time I watched our little Elara being poked and prodded. It's something I will always be uncomfortable with, but an unsettling truth is that over time I got used to it in many ways. This is a theme I will return to throughout this story—which, by the way, does have a happy ending for us—that we as humans are equipped with the tools necessary to adapt and go through adversity with massive internal strength. But I didn't feel it that day. That day, I heard Elara scream. She screamed in fear and discomfort as they sedated her to administer the MRI. Is this anguish she experienced the cost of doing business—an unsettling emotional means to an end? Sure. Is it traumatizing to see it happen? Damn right it is, especially at first. If I could have downed a stiff drink or puffed on a funny cigarette at that very moment, I definitely would have. God, it sucks seeing kids in distress when they don't understand why they are suffering from situations out of their control.

*What I didn't know then is that our bodies are equipped to handle such things, and many times, it is the fear of the unknown that is worse than the reality we do know. I was taught this lesson many times on this journey.*

We arrived at Kelowna General Hospital at seven that morning. I remember it being a huge inconvenience for the four of us. I mean, it was Christmas Eve Day, and we had to wake Elara up so early to get there on time. That mindset of inconvenience revealed our perception that we really didn't think it was too big of a deal. I believed Elara was fine. It was around four in the afternoon when the nice doctor and nurse sat down with us to share the news. That moment changed each of our lives forever.

Candy immediately started crying, but it took me a while for the emotion to come over me. I remember just sitting there trying to understand. I was definitely experiencing shock, and a feeling of numbness moved through me that sometimes returns when I think back on that day. Perhaps that will take some therapy to shake loose at a future time. Or maybe it's a memory I am supposed to keep—an emotional scar. This day presented a series of never-ending questions, each answered with the same response: *I don't know.*

From an outside perspective, if someone viewed the sociology of our four different reactions over the first 20 minutes or so, I am sure we were fascinating—two men and two women of different ages and life experiences. Our commonality is that we all love Elara, yet in our own special and unique way. We were all reacting to something we were helpless to do anything about. And there she was, still a touch groggy and grouchy from the MRI. My stepson and I distracted her off and on as she received cuddles from her mom and was then passed over to Mimi—Candy—for more loving. She had a popsicle every once in a while that afternoon, and that was cute because it wasn't a particular treat she was used to. We watched as she ate them in wonder, completely oblivious to the emotion the adults were feeling, as her distress was now in the past.

A woman came in identifying herself as a social worker. I had a preconceived notion about what social workers do, and it sure wasn't this, so I was immediately confused. In my head, social workers dealt with counselling or other personal or family matters outside of a hospital setting. It just shows how clueless I was about how things work and the amazing emotional infrastructure we do have behind the scenes for people. She came in and informed us the kids were booked into Ronald McDonald House for the following Friday. They had an appointment with a surgeon that morning as well. Her logistical skills were exemplary as she gave Elara's parents information on many things, from funding to geographical directions. I was stunned and full of questions. The first was the one some of us went to right away: *Was this mass cancerous?* They didn't know.

Before we even left that room, one of the kid's friends organized and uploaded a GoFundMe[1] for them. I wondered: *Was that truly necessary?* It turns out it definitely was. *Aren't we moving a little fast here? We don't even know what we're dealing with.* Much of the time, I am extremely grateful for my logical mind, but sometimes, it just doesn't serve me. After a time, I just sat in the windowsill of the hospital room we were in, and tears began flowing down my face. *How could someone so small and playful be so sick? Is she sick? Did she just become sick in that instant?* If so, she was the happiest sick kid I'd ever seen.

***I came to learn that many kids go through illness much better than adults do because they are always so in the moment. Theirs is a natural existence of being present.***

---

[1] https://ca.gofundme.com

They aren't worried about mortgage payments or what they are going to eat for dinner that night. They look at, react to, and only feel what is directly in front of them. Elara's default is happy. She always wants to be happy. So, how could she be sick? When I am sick, which is rare, I get whiney and think I am going to die. I dwell on my suffering over and over while distracting myself with comic books or the internet or video games, hoping to be waited on by my wife, which by the way, she has little patience for. Elara just wants to play with her toys and feed me her squishy baby food. I contemplated how in the world we would possibly get through such a situation. Looking back, I wish I had taken advice from Elara during this time and just stayed present more. Instead, it took me months and a whole lot of misguided emotions and a waste of time and effort on many occasions to learn what she already knew: *Take it as it comes*, silly man. This is a handy skill I learned going through this experience, one I cannot emphasize enough for anyone going through something big like this. Even though it's hard, try to decide to forget about the future and just take each moment as it comes. Everything else will unfold in due time. That skill helped me countless times before this ordeal was over.

We left the Kelowna General hospital around six o'clock on Christmas Eve. Candy rode with the kids and the baby. The plan was to go back to our place, Elara's second home. Since being a newborn, Elara has constantly spent time at our house. As the kids eased into becoming parents, it became a place of safety and support for them as well. This was fine as wine to Candy and me because we loved having them over, even during difficult times. I went to the store to pick up a few things. I don't remember everything I bought, but I did make sure to include a box of the same popsicles Elara was devouring at the hospital. Once home, we got down to business and started comparing notes. My parents and our younger son and wife came over. They were all wrecks at first, but God bless her, Elara wouldn't have it, and she took over. She ran around, making us all laugh, being the life of the party. She sat at the *Frozen 2* vanity Candy and I got her—it sang to her, and she loved that.

We started asking difficult questions trying to put two and two together. We always delighted in how Elara ran on her tiptoes so much: *Was this internal mass the reason she did that? Is this why she hates the car seat so much?* When she learned to crawl, she kind of had this cute little side shuffle she did that made everyone howl with laughter: *Was it because of the friend growing inside her, making her shift?* That night was, surprisingly, a really good time. I'm convinced it was because we were all in some sort of denial. Upon reflection, it was simply the rest of us taking a page out of Elara's book without even knowing it. We were present and in the moment, and it wasn't possible not to have a good time because Elara was having a great time. She stopped at nothing to make sure we joined her. It felt like an 80s pop song with lyrics making claims that we only have tonight, so let's make the best of it; advice I always felt led to trouble if followed. But not that night. Instead, we embraced the joy that Elara was experiencing because she knew that's what we all needed. It was an incredibly fun night. Of course, it was not to last, and the other shoe of reality dropped not even eight hours later.

# II

# Awakening

If there is one thing this entire situation taught me, it's that I need to be more like Elara. If I could feel, see, and experience the world in a couple of key areas through the mind of a small child the way she does, I believe that the rest of my adult life would be a lot more satisfying. Boy, oh boy, I sure want to be like Elara!

I first began to notice this delayed epiphany the day we arrived at BC Children's hospital. Candy and I drove to Vancouver on December 26th to prepare for the kids' arrival; they were flying in the next morning. We wanted to know the geography of where we were spending the next week or so. I say a week because I truly thought the mass behind Elara's tailbone was a cyst. It wasn't a far stretch for a few reasons. The first, of course, was denial. In both my head and heart, there was no way this mass could be cancerous. I used the following justifications: *She is fine, look at her, she's happy all the time; if she were sick, she would show it in the way she behaves; her energy levels are through the roof, or look how much she is eating!*

I had these authentic opinions about Elara and believed they were one hundred percent true. I easily used them to make myself believe she was okay, all things considered. I believed this so strongly because I've heard about cysts occurring like this in all sorts of people, both kids and adults, and having them removed was a fairly normal occurrence. Personally, I have three friends who have gone through this very thing. Candy and I had a trip to Disneyland and Palm Springs planned beginning January 5th, and at the time, it never crossed our minds that we would have to cancel our trip. We, of course, intended to make sure the kids were okay dealing with the situation. But we felt a strong possibility that by the fifth, we could jet set while Elara was safely healing at home. The kids never asked us to join them on this journey, and I am not sure they would have if we had not decided to right away. Asking people to put their lives on hold is not something that comes easy to the best of us, I am sure. But it's weird and even kind of serendipitous that Candy and I didn't even discuss going along to Vancouver to be a support. We both assumed it was happening instinctually and instantaneously. It was never a question.

When Candy and I arrived at the airport—more on that facility later as we aren't done with that place by a **LONGSHOT**—on December 27th to pick the kids up, it was stressful. There were the usual stresses, like being at an unfamiliar international airport under construction, trying to find the correct terminal, and looking for the kids as they arrived surrounded by thousands of other travellers. All that was stressful enough, never mind the fact that as soon as they got in the SUV, we had to drive directly to Elara's appointment. The only thing we knew for sure about where we were going was that it contained fear and uncertainty. Lots of stress that day, to say the least.

Whenever Candy and I take road trips to unfamiliar lands, we have defined roles: I am the driver, and she is my *Navi Ho*. Back in the day when I was a kid, my dad sometimes made the drive from Kelowna to Vancouver hauling materials for the company he worked for. Sometimes, I would tag along. I will be forever grateful for those trips as they, not only provided nine-year-old me with a set of new surroundings, but every time we went to the big city, it expanded my young mind. During those journeys, I had a **VERY** important job as the navigator. Technology was very different back then with no GPS or Google Maps. There were only paper maps. And it was nine-year-old Mike's job to sit in the passenger seat assisting with directions while dad, also named Mike, maneuvered a giant flatbed truck loaded with materials through the narrow streets of Vancouver. I loved being his navigator because it made me feel important. When Candy and I got together, the road trip roles naturally developed; I would drive, she would navigate. But calling her a navigator was not our style. Instead, she became my *Navi Ho*. I won't go any further into the explanation; you are all big boys and girls and can probably fill in the blanks as to why one might think it's a clever nickname. Is it politically correct? Probably not. But we think it's kind of adorable, and it's one of those little relationship-shorthand details people have. However, it gets less cute when stress is added to the trip.

When the kids arrived, many emotions came with them. One thing I learned during our ordeal is that, sometimes, people process and react to things very differently. I tried hard not to show how I felt to the kids if at all possible. I just didn't think it would help the situation, and I viewed myself as a piece of equipment or a tool to assist the kids rather than hinder them. And then there was Elara.

*The thing about Elara is that her default is usually happy.*
*That is what she wants to be.*

Unless she's in pain or doesn't understand what is going on around her, or she doesn't get her way, Elara is pretty much an angel behaviour-wise. I am so grateful for that.

That morning as we rushed to pack her into her car seat and put the luggage in the cargo hold, she was pretty zen, all things considered. She lit up when she saw Candy and me; a lot was going on, and she was content to be with her family. She loves when we are all together. If only I had taken a page from her book that morning, maybe the edge of some of that stress would have been taken away.

Candy and I scoped the route to the hospital the day before, and it was a fairly simple drive taking less than half an hour with minimal ramps and exits. But with the added stress baggage, the journey was mentally more difficult for me than it usually would be. First off, everyone was talking. It was then when I began learning how to tune out conversations while driving a motor vehicle but also be present enough to answer someone who was talking directly to me. I'm sure it's a skill that bus drivers, cabbies, or proficient Uber drivers have mastered, but that day, I realized I was a novice. I am happy to say it is now indeed a skill I have added to my repertoire. I also had the extra mental weight that there was a baby in the car as a passenger. Not only was she the child I care for far more than nearly everything on this earth, but she was also a sick one. One of the struggles I've had driving in foreign cities is that sometimes I'm too hesitant. It could be when I change lanes or make certain turns, and what I found out in my experience is that hesitancy, both on the road and in life in general, can lead to missed opportunities. Hesitancy while driving can mean taking longer to get to the destination, missing an exit, or causing an accident.

Thank goodness I was focused that morning, and our journey was uneventful. We got to the hospital with Candy's expert Navi Ho guidance supporting us, and I parked the car. On the outside, other than being on a large campus with multiple buildings and a bit of happy signage, BC Children's hospital looks like most medical facilities I've seen over my lifetime. We later learned about the organization's true beauty and how massively powerful and unique that place actually is. But there, in the parking lot that morning, I became totally task-oriented. I parked by the correct building. I paid for parking. I helped unload. I looked for signs indicating where we were heading. I think part of it was that if all I had to think about was what to do next, I wouldn't have to face the reality of Elara being sick. After all, there was too much to do, and this kept me distracted from what I didn't want to believe. We entered the building, and I immediately understood this was a very different place. First of all, I noticed the way it was decorated. It was...happy? Perhaps not quite the right word, but yes, it kind of was. For a hospital, it was lighter, not just in physical brightness but in its energy; more so than any medical facility I've ever encountered. The people at the information desk actually smiled at us when we asked for directions, as did many of the staff walking by us. And they weren't pity smiles because we had an adorable sick kid in our party; people at BC Children's just smiled at each other. Cool. The first stop was the oncology ward, which was on the eighth floor. We checked in and were sent to the outpatient section to wait for our consultation. *The oncology ward is for all growths; this won't be cancer,* I told myself. The waiting room was rad. It had wonderful distractions for kids of all ages, from toys and crafts of all kinds to multiple Xboxes and PlayStations. It was painted in happy colours. Elara loved it. As we waited, she ran around the room overloaded with all the fun stimuli that surrounded her. There was a translucent wall, and she and I ran back and forth, looking at each other through the glass. At that moment, I put up my first social media post about our situation:

*Today at BC Children's hospital,*
*the emotions were literally everywhere.*
*Some really hard truths and really, really big fears.*
*But you know what?*
*Elara, my sweet granddaughter,*
*is a fighter and will default to happy*
*as much as possible. Here is an example...*

I was speaking about a cute video I posted of Elara looking at me through the window in the waiting room. She was jumping down and running around to see me on the other side. The camera moved back to look through the window just in time to catch her leaping into my arms with her gorgeous hair flowing behind her. While her parents and grandparents were worried sick and scattered, Elara was present and just simply happy, taking things as they came. I now strive to do the same and wish I knew that trick back then. I recognize that I have already mentioned this a few times during this narrative—and I probably will again—this skill I speak of has changed my life.

Soon after, we were introduced to Elara's team. Team? Yes, that's how it works. She had a team of people assigned to her. And not just that day; some of Elara's team members will be with her for the next 18 years. We met her social worker, and as I mentioned earlier, this was a career role I wasn't completely clear about. She introduced herself to us and let us know that her role was to assist us with nearly anything she could, and the scope of that was vast. Need a letter written to an employer, benefit company, or an airline or hotel? That's her. Having a hard time dealing and need some counselling? She sets it up, and fast. Need a parking pass, housing at Ronald McDonald House, or Easter Seals? She's on it. Wow. Cool. I wish all health care situations had someone like her. She was like a powerful concierge for a critical situation.

It was also on that first day we realized some limitations that family dynamics expose. While given massive respect, *the grandparents* often become an afterthought in situations like these. When not admitted to the hospital, the kids and Elara were given a place to stay. However, not being the parents or legal guardians, Candy and I were left to find our own accommodations. There was no provision for support family members—not that it would have stopped us because we would have figured it out.

Next, we met someone who became very special to Candy and me, Elara's nurse clinician, Suzanne, and if we have our way, she will be a lifelong friend. Suzanne is Elara's head nurse. She organizes and quarterbacks nearly everything that happens with Elara, from tests and the first analysis of said tests to meetings and treatments, and she will continue to do so through years to come.

*She is also what I like to refer to as a low-flying angel, someone who is so amazing and beautiful in spirit; they are difficult to see as a mere human.*

By the way, Candy is one of these angels as well. My wife is a powerhouse who has accomplished a lot of very cool things in her life, and she is just getting started! Her goal is to change the world. It was immediately apparent to Candy and me that we had someone in our corner who would care for Elara like she was one of her own. We knew right away that she would do **EVERYTHING** in her power to be there for us. I cannot express enough the phenom this woman is! More than once, her empathetic heart and brilliant mind stopped my life from spinning out of control. Suzanne always let us know what was happening. The fact that she doesn't just do this for us, but dozens of other families, simultaneously, blows me away.

Behind the scenes during the few days since the revelation at Kelowna General, there was clearly a lot of thought and work put into Elara's situation. Since receiving Elara's info, many people at BC Children's worked hard over Christmas, no less, on our behalf. Whoever those people were, I am grateful for them. The next step was meeting some impressive surgeons who consulted with us on the removal of the mass, which would take place around New Year's. As soon as the surgery was booked, they would let us know the exact date and time. I was impressed they came to this conclusion before we even met, and I continued to believe Elara had a fairly *routine* cyst that needed to be removed and all would be just fine. *Don't worry, Candy, Disneyland, here we come*—a much-needed rest after a stressful autumn, which included Candy losing her father after a long health battle. Oh, how wrong I was!

Of course, Elara stole the hearts of all the members on her team. She tends to do that wherever she goes being that she is the cutest human ever born on this earth. No, I am not biased at all! I soon realized it wasn't just Elara's cuteness that won them over, but that is the culture of BC Children's Hospital. They really, really care, and not just about the physical welfare of their patients but also about the negative implications that illness can create. In our experience, their goal is to cure disease and ailments, but also heal unwanted side effects they bring along with them.

Again, looking back, I wish I would have held my stress back and just been in the moment and grateful to be with my family the way Elara was. The following days, weeks, and months provided many opportunities to be scared or stressed about real things. I have since learned that life's real issues carry enough stuff to worry about. Why add even more stress with the fear of the unknown? That statement might be easier said than done, but like many things I have learned, it is a skill that can be developed. And I met a living example of this truth: his name is Tim.

I met Tim at Ronald McDonald House the day the kids arrived in Vancouver after our appointment at the hospital. RMH is a facility on the grounds of BC Children's Hospital that can house over 70 families from out of town needing extended treatments or stays at while there. It is a phenomenal place. Late that afternoon following our appointment, my stepson and I received a tour around the beautiful facility by one of the friendly administrators. She showed us its various features and coached us about the culture they are striving to achieve for the dozens of families staying there. Then, entering one of the four eating and kitchens areas, I rounded a corner and, quite literally, bumped into a very friendly Englishman who was also staying there. He immediately asked if we were new to RMH, and we let him know that we had indeed just arrived. Tim introduced himself, and we had a 10-minute conversation, whereby we got to know each other a bit. He gave us some general insights and tips about staying at the facility, and we exchanged stories about what brought us there. At the end of our conversation, we traded contact info so that we could talk more later.

He and his son normally reside in Penticton, which is coincidentally just an hour's drive from Kelowna, where Candy and I live. Tim's son, an amazing boy named Wills, was also dealing with cancer-related issues. Tim shared a lot of tidbits of knowledge and advice with me, and I got to know him over the next few months. I was blown away by his resilience, given what he had gone through. I thought my family's situation was hard, and it was, but there is always perspective. While we had a plan about how things would transpire for Elara, Tim's family situation was a lot more complex. Wills had a variety of uncertain outcomes attached to them. To this day, over a year since we have been back home and after a very short reprieve, Tim and Wills are still staying at Ronald McDonald House, battling at BC Children's hospital.

How does he do it? One day at a time. Tim was such a help to me those first few weeks. He was so generous, sharing the knowledge he gained over the past year. It's so difficult knowing they are still living one procedure at a time. I have learned not to feel guilty that we are home and Elara has healed while they are still down there. However, I am mindful to regard our situation with gratitude and theirs with deep compassion. Tim and Wills are amazing examples of individuals making the best of managing adversity. They play soccer—the original football—whenever they can and take advantage of every single moment of reprieve they have.

There are a few other things I learned about being exposed to Ronald McDonald House. The first is, it's important not to take on the energy of other families staying there. This advice was given to me by a few folks, including doctors and other patients' families who previously stayed there. With love, many warned me I would encounter people who could potentially add some unnecessary drama to our situation if we got sucked into what they were dealing with. One very wise person pulled me aside and told me: *Their problems are not your problems; do your best not to take them on.* This made sense and became apparent nearly instantly.

Anytime a group of people gather, dramatic social dynamics inevitably pop up. In my experience, this is a continual challenge that RMH faces. Some of the people staying there are emotionally compromised, and they are roommates who, although unintentionally, make things more difficult for those around them. Of course, it's understandable, but it can make waves, nonetheless. These behaviours range and manifest in all sorts of ways. For some parents, their child's condition triggers fear and an instinct to protect their son or daughter from anyone who might even just approach them. For other folks, many who stayed at the facility for long periods of time, fussiness or frustration was expressed concerning how others don't do things up to their standards.

This happened the day after I had my tour. Candy and I came over to RMH to visit the kids and Elara. I went down to the kitchen, where they allocated fridge space for personal food and a community pantry that families could use as needed. I was loading the dishwasher—which reminded me of the same industrial unit at the summer camp I visited in grade nine—when a woman appeared out of nowhere and began sternly reprimanding me. Unbeknownst to me, she watched me like a hawk and gruffly corrected the way I was putting the plates and coffee mugs into the dishwasher. Taken aback and not knowing what else to do, I apologized to her. She rolled her eyes and walked away. Someone who witnessed the exchange came over and began soothing me, letting me know the woman's situation, which was heartbreaking. She was a mother of three and a single mom at that. She and her sick child had already been at RMH for nine months, while her other kids stayed back at home. She had only seen her other children a handful of times these past few months. Empathy immediately washed over any negative emotions I might have been feeling, and all I could do was feel bad for her.

Sometimes I watched the pods of people staying there, and it felt a bit like high school. There were cliques. I learned that it's up to us to try and regulate our emotional intelligence while spending time there and look out for people who share that same ideal. Tim was one of those people. And the staff of RMH was **CONSTANTLY** doing things to keep the atmosphere as light and positive as possible. They did everything from facilitating music nights to concerts or providing video game competitions in the massive community room in the centre of the facility. They offered cooking events and massage to the parents in an attempt to help ease their burden. There were also displays showcasing items donated to the families staying there—these are tiny examples of what this place does for those who stay at RMH. Add the multiple playrooms filled with goodies for all ages and the art and music rooms, and it doesn't take much to realize that this is a place built to give children as much normalcy as possible while going through their health challenges. It never occurred to me how important Ronald McDonald House is, even though I have seen commercials and advertisements for fundraisers for the place since I was a boy. It was only when my family needed it when I realized that both gratefulness and the fierce desire to support such places will always be with me moving forward.

I was awakened to one other lesson that first week living in Vancouver—one that would take months to sink in completely. On the second or third morning, arriving at RMH to visit Elara and the kids, I did a double take as I walked by the front desk. The logo of my very favourite hockey team was displayed in a plastic frame. I am a **GIGANTIC** Los Angeles Kings fan. Some people see how devoted I am to the team and back away, thinking I'm some kind of freak—I even have a crown tattooed on my back! As I'm writing these words, sitting in my home office, I take a moment to glance around at all the Kings' stuff on my walls. It makes me smile really big.

Since childhood, I made the trek to Vancouver at least once a season to watch my Kings play the Canucks. That morning, I saw that a family who owns season seats to the Canucks donated tickets for the game scheduled a couple of nights later. Guess who the team was? Yup, the LA Kings. And how could I have a chance to secure those tickets? All I had to do was put my name in a box that sat beside the display on the counter. Without a second thought, I put my name in, along with the kids' room information. I didn't think much of it, even when someone called saying they chose us as the winners of the tickets. Candy told my stepson and me to have a great time as Elara and her mom came over to our hotel inside the Vancouver International Airport—more on that place later—for a carpet picnic and possible swim in the pool that overlooked the departure lounge.

On the sky train heading to Rogers Arena, I began to feel some guilt surfacing. Here I was in Vancouver, going to see a hockey game, while my granddaughter was days away from a *MAJOR* surgery. Should I be doing this? Am I a villain for doing this? Shouldn't I be forgoing such things to spend more time with Elara? Of course, I had fun at the game. Drew Doughty, my favourite King, saw me cheering for him from the stands and pointed at me. Was I a jerk for enjoying that moment? Unfortunately, for a while, I felt a lot of needless guilt whenever I did something I enjoyed during this ordeal, and it took me some time to come up with an answer to this question. Elara was potentially mortally ill, but did that mean my life should stop in its tracks? It took some reflection for me to balance the ethical scale loaded up on both sides that night.

Look, I can only share my perspective and the personal insights I gained; I understand others may not see it the way that I do. What I learned was right for me, and when I made peace with it, I was **MUCH** more effective as a support for my family. I firmly believe that in order to be strong for others around me, I need to stay strong by filling my cup, which includes doing things I like to do. The good fortune of that hockey game falling in our laps was a way I could do that. And when I looked for them, all sorts of opportunities presented themselves to us here and there that would put a few precious drops back into our rapidly leaking cups.

I had to warm up to not feeling guilty about such things, but once I truly awakened to that idea, I realized how essential it was that I found things Candy and I could do to keep our spirits strong. The ripple of that strength translated into us being the supportive force our family needed—some of those things we did together, and some, alone. The importance of finding that personal truth was that it kept me from losing who I am during this unprecedented process.

If I could provide any food for thought to those going through something similar, I would share the example of an airplane cabin that begins to depressurize in a state of emergency. Instead of reading or playing your game boy or listening to music, pay attention to the safety demonstration at the front of the cabin before takeoff. The flight attendant will explain that if the plane cabin depressurizes during the flight, masks will fall from compartments above. They will then instruct you to put your mask on first before helping anyone else—including your children—and that makes sense.

It was easy to forget that lesson going through what we did, and we almost became martyrs for Elara, not realizing that, in the end, it simply wouldn't help. And if I had looked to Elara instead, I would have instantly seen that, outside of difficult hospital situations, she did everything she could just to enjoy life. Had I used that ultimate example early on in our journey, I would have found many other ways to release moments of tension and stress while avoiding unnecessary distress along the way.

# III

# Distractions and Reminders

I have often wondered what kind of world it would be if all humans had a sign hanging from their necks with a quick synopsis of their current mental state. Like if someone in my life was having a conversation with me, maybe about a movie they watched or a date they just went on, and I could look down and see that they are feeling something **REALLY** different from what they're saying. Perhaps they are sad, mad, or scared, but I would never know if they weren't wearing their sign. That's what the cat ears I wore on my head for four months were to me; they were a sign saying I was in distress.

A few days into our journey, a care package arrived from someone. Elara being sick sounded an alarm bell so loudly that many people were mobilized to send our family all sorts of things, big and small, with the intention to help ease the burden a bit. There were dozens of things, from stuffed animals to gift cards for groceries to clothes for the baby and many other items. It was awesome to see how many people supported our family this way. One afternoon, very early during our stay in Vancouver, Candy and I arrived to pick the kids up, and one of these care packages was open with its contents lying on the bed. I zeroed in on one of the items immediately; it was a headband with ears covered in a leopard print. I have seen these around in the world, usually worn by tweens trying to add an element of cute animal to their look. Without hesitation, I grabbed the headband and put it on to see what Elara's reaction would be. She smiled really big right away and said *Mow!* with delight. Mow is the word she and I like to call back and forth to each other, usually when we drive into the townhouse complex where Candy and I live. We have a cat named Drew—named after Drew Doughty of the Kings, of course, who Elara is fascinated by—and I think she identifies our house with her. So, Mow is what she always exclaimed and still does from time to time. When she yelled it after seeing me put the headband on, I knew I had something. I made an instantaneous decision:

> *Other than sleeping or showering,*
> *I would not remove the cat ears until our*
> *family's ordeal was over.*
> *I have no idea why I made that decision.*

But like most things, decisions like that end up making sense after some time goes by. At first, my family didn't know what to make of my resolution to wear the cat ears day in and day out—except for Elara. She loved it. Many times, I would enter a room and she would happily exclaim *Mow!* Sometimes she would take them off my head and put them on hers, but she would always give them back. As for the rest of the family, they just became desensitized to the adorable cat ears on Pa's head.

I wore the ears wherever we went, no matter what clothes I had on. As far as I was concerned, they went with everything. When Candy posted stories on her social media and included me in them, someone always commented: *What's with the ears?* Her response was always the same: *He wears them for Elara.* For me, it didn't take long to stop noticing the looks I got when out in public. But I did get a lot of them. I have no clue what thoughts some people had about me wearing the ears, but that didn't matter to me. However, I did come up with an instantaneous response if anyone asked me about them—it made me think about the idea of wearing signs around our necks all the time. When someone commented or asked me about the ears, here's how the conversation nearly always went...

Someone would say: *Nice ears* or *I like your ears.* They had various looks from curious to sarcastic on their faces while commenting. My response would always be same: *Yeah, you really like them?* I would ask them this to provide them with the opportunity to disengage if they wanted to, but they rarely did. Mostly they would answer: *Ya, they are cute,* or something like that. At that point, I would continue: *Can I tell you why I wear these ears?* To which they would usually say, with hesitation: *Okaaaay...*

It was then that, unless Elara was with us, I would take out my phone and show the person my home screen, displaying a photo of Elara at the winter block party taken moments before she captivated the band playing that gorgeous winter night. She looks like a baby angel in that photo with lights and white snow surrounding her; her dark hair is cascading down her back from under her toque, and her eyes are glowing above her dazzling, infectious smile. I would then go on to tell them: *This is my granddaughter. On Christmas Eve, we found out she had a tumour the size of my fist right behind her tailbone. We are living down here in Vancouver as a family for the next few months as she is being taken care of at BC Children's Hospital. I wear these ears because she loves them, and every time someone asks me about them, it gives me the opportunity to tell the story and think of her—now we can both send up positive thoughts for her and the hope that she heals and gets better.*

I tried to keep track, and I think over the four-plus months, I must have said that at least a few dozen times, maybe more.

As you might imagine, the responses I got were all over the place. A few individuals seemed to feel awkward and said: *Oh, okay*, without any other discourse, but those experiences were actually few and far between. The vast majority of people were blown away by my unexpected response and many responded in amazing ways. Some asked if they could pray for Elara right then and there. Most agreed to send up some positive vibes and say something encouraging. I felt a little guilty when a server at a restaurant asked about the cat ears because many times it led to us getting a meal discounted or comped, which was never my intention in any way. However, it was greatly appreciated, of course.

A few times, those ears transitioned into some really meaningful, emotional moments. A few of the conversations ended up being with people who were or knew cancer survivors themselves, or they had an experience of some kind with BC Children's Hospital. We met one man while climbing down a flight of stairs from a downtown Vancouver street to the entrance of an underground mall who ended up telling us through tears about his personal experience with cancer as a child and what it means for him to be a survivor. I cannot adequately describe the hope he gave me that day. Those cat ears led to the shedding of many tears of hope. They were literally a sign I wore, signalling people that I was not okay. And I wasn't...especially at first. But as time went by, I got better. Stronger. I started to heal as Elara healed in the ways she needed to. Don't get me wrong, I am not saying that my healing was tied to hers—although it did help, of course—but more that my healing was a convergence of truths discovered, lessons learned, and the support of others I relied upon.

Candy is fond of a description she uses of our personal development journey, saying:

*Sometimes we have to take ourselves down to the studs in order to rebuild ourselves stronger.*

And while I would never, ever wish what we went through on anyone, I do appreciate what the experience taught me. My hope is those learnings stay with me forever. A few weeks after nearly accidentally killing the family—the trick is to go **AROUND** the berm, but more on that later—I was starting to embrace the realization I touched on last chapter, which was that I needed to do some *normal* things to stay sane. So, I had our younger son and his wife bring up my guitar on one of their visits, and our Nintendo Switch so Candy and I could play games during the downtime; another thing this experience taught me is that there is a lot of downtime going through an ordeal like this. There were also moments of extreme suddenness and dizzying activity, but they were usually followed by a stretch of recovery time when waiting is, unfortunately, all that could be done. So, I began meditating and doing yoga. While at the hospital, I took the stairs up and down from the eighth floor to get my blood pumping instead of using the elevator. And every morning, I put those cat ears on my head, and as time went by, they began to be a source of power to me—a kind guide, like a totem. While there were still many ups and downs, they became much more manageable. I started putting writings and videos up on my social media, not only to update people, but for me to stay accountable. Many people responded, and while thankful for their support and encouragement, it was secondary because I did it for me. That very strength serves me even months after the fact when I get caught up in the little things that present and can hijack my emotions. I now reframe things, like something not going right at work, or hearing an unflattering comment about me in a completely different way;

I remember to be mindful of my learnings and become present again. I am so grateful for the timing of how things transpired because I now understand that we were completely prepared when life gave this unexpected test without even knowing it.

Of course, this was not something I understood in the moment. Until this point, all I knew was that my granddaughter was critically ill, and dealing with the unpredictable unfolding of that outcome was a teacher I didn't expect. She went through her surgery, and the tumour was analyzed and deemed cancerous, making it official that our stay would be much longer than originally thought. The terrifying highs and dizzying lows of the early days of the ordeal were unlike anything I had ever encountered to that point in my life. We tried to plan with the best intentions, but things swung back and forth like a ship in a storm. There was the worry of getting there, then getting settled, and the dread of the unknown, then meeting with the doctors and experiencing the comfort of having a plan. We experienced surgery day and the horrors that came along with it to the monumental relief and gratefulness of recovery. Finally, we received the gutshot of finding out the tumour was cancerous. We prepared for and moved through her first round of Chemo and said our final goodbye to her treatments after being told they were done and knowing she would be fine. This experience was a crash course in learning to deal with rapidly changing events.

*I literally could not hang my hat on anything because the hat rack kept disappearing into the floor, only to appear in another part of the room.*

But it fills me with gratitude now to be conscious of the many things that counteract such trials—the fact that we live in a place with systems to deal with these things and have

30

teams of people to help. And we didn't have to be alone if we didn't want to be. Incredibly, medical science has progressed to optimistically manage and deal with something that would likely have been fatal decades ago. It became obvious that a community can mobilize, come forward, and assist in a plethora of ways when the chips are down.

The most impactful revelation for me was that my body and spirit are much stronger than I ever thought they were or even could be. I now see the blessings these lessons taught to me throughout this entire journey. Of course, there are times when blessings show up as a kick to the teeth. That was what went on inside of me. Most people would have no idea of the internal struggle and learning I was experiencing unless, of course, they understood the sign on my head—a set of cat ears made of plastic and fabric.

# IV

# Freedom

After being in Vancouver for a few weeks, the alarm bell sounded, *both* on social media and other traditional ways of spreading news, as to why we were there. As a result, I thought we would be inundated with calls, texts, and emails from concerned friends and family. And we were, just not always in the way I expected.

Going through life, I have consciously evolved in the way I interact with people, specifically in regards to confrontation. I was somewhere in my 30s when I really started making conscious decisions not to sweep things under the rug, even when tempted to. I remember having the urge to ignore someone I knew and behave in this way when something difficult happened to them. For example, perhaps there was a time when a friend's wife left him, or maybe someone I knew had their business publicly collapse, or a friend had someone close to them die suddenly. If I saw them across the street, my response would be not to alert them I was there. Sometimes, I would even turn around and walk the other way. I know now that I am not the only one who has acted like this, but I felt like I was back then.

I think that if I didn't know what to say or knew of a way to help, I chose not to say or do anything at all. I justified that behaviour in all sorts of ways, telling myself: *They are going through so much right now, I don't want to remind them of it, or*

*It would suck to make them cry and ruin their day.* But the truth is that it was my fear stopping me from approaching them because I wanted to avoid feeling awkward. After all, who likes feeling awkward? I don't know if I have extra sensitivity to that feeling or not. But I do know that when I watched the TV show, *The Office*, which was filled with awkward moments, I was constantly cringing, sometimes to the point of turning the volume down or fast forwarding past the situation. The writers of comedies like *The Office* or *Curb Your Enthusiasm* are masters at creating those cringe-worthy moments to get a laugh. But what about when they happen in real life? What about when something that sucks happens to someone I know, and from my point of view, there was very little I could say or do to support them? Many times, I simply avoided them.

Then, as I entered my third decade on this earth, I consciously got in the habit of doing the opposite because I didn't enjoy the feeling I experienced when I turned my back on uncomfortable situations. The shorthand Candy and I use to describe this is staying in the fire.

**It involves being aware of a potentially heated situation and taking it head-on, no matter how hot it gets, even if it means getting singed.**

Once that decision was made, it became easier. I find that when I commit to staying in the fire, a couple of things come to fruition. First, the confrontation is usually not nearly as bad as I imagined it would be. Talking about the elephant in the room almost instantly eliminates any awkward feeling. I remember this very thing while talking to a friend who was publicly cheated on a few years back. The moment he and I started talking about it, all fear associated with having the conversation suddenly vanished. We actually spent little time talking about the infraction itself; he let me know what was up with him and how he was dealing with it, and then we focused more on catching up.

The second thing I learned by creating the habit of confronting awkward situations was that most of the time, the person I stayed in the fire with appreciated it and let me know they did—literally the opposite of what I feared. There were also times when it led to opportunities. It may be because I am not alone within these human tendencies, burying my head in the sand like an ostrich and ignoring what's going on up on the surface. I found that most often the person appreciates the conversation and that I acknowledged their situation. Other times, they welcomed my advice and support, sometimes even professionally, which created opportunities for them and me at the same time. However, until Elara got sick, and we were suddenly uprooted, I never felt I was on the other side of the equation. I never knowingly experienced people putting their heads down and walking the other way when they saw me.

Of course, some people reached out to us once the holiday season was over and we were into 2020; some had advice, both good and bad. Some offered support, financial and otherwise. One gal offered an empty house to stay in while we were in Vancouver, which was, unfortunately too far away from the kids staying at Ronald McDonald House. But some of the people I would have labeled having a close relationship with before, completely ghosted me... people I worked side by side with for years... people I've spent considerable time and effort supporting through difficult situations of their own. Some remained quiet for a while, then broke down and called or texted after a month or two. Then, there were those who I considered to be great friends who didn't reach out at all. I quickly discovered what it felt like to be on the other side of *staying in the fire.*

I don't harbour resentment to anyone who felt the need to keep their distance—at least not anymore. I've been in their shoes and understand how it feels not to have the courage to reach out because they feel uneasy, even now that we are home. I reached out to a few of them to release the tension, and because I missed them! Some levelled with me, saying they just didn't know what to say, and they felt like schmucks. And yet, there are a couple who still said nothing at all, perhaps hoping that things would soon return to *normal.*

**It's quite fascinating to me how each person in my life reacted to the news when I take away the highly charged emotions of the situation.**

Did it hurt? Sometimes. Some relationships are forever fractured from my side, but I have found gratitude within this. Experiencing how they responded to our situation has shown me that if they cannot stay in the fire at this point in their life, I might be better off keeping them at arm's length, knowing I am unable to count on them when the chips are down. While this made me sad temporarily, it is also very freeing. I am grateful to know and understand where they are within their tolerance of emotional fire pertaining to me.

And then there was another group of people, whose reaction to our family's situation was not anticipated. The gal who offered us a freaking house to live in was an acquaintance within our social circle, who I saw not more than a couple of times a year. We would have accepted her offer in a second if we could have as it would have saved us over 10,000 dollars! And she wasn't the only one. Many people who Candy and I would have classified as acquaintances before we left for Vancouver very nearly instantly reached out to us. People we only knew a little bit literally forced their support on us. So many facets of this overwhelmed and impacted me. First, let's start with the GoFundMe that raised over 10,000 dollars within a few days—five figures! This was before we even knew the scope of Elara's illness. Holy Smokes. We were dumbfounded and grateful that people would do that for the kids. We wondered if that much was necessary, and it turns out, it sure was! As the same gal who offered us the house said to me: *Cancer is expensive!*

Once revealed that we would be in Vancouver for at least four months, the community around us responded. The GoFundMe for Elara raised over 21,000 dollars before all was said and done. Local media covered our story and pointed people to the fundraiser. Please let me state right now in big, bold letters on behalf of our family **THANK YOU, THANK YOU, THANK YOU** to everyone who donated, promoted, or raised money in that GoFundMe. We understand that not every family going through these types of situations is fortunate enough to have people rally around them as we did. During our journey, we met a lot of families going through similar, if not more difficult adversities than we were, and they did not have as much support. Complete strangers donated and reached out to us. Guys in the guild of the Star Wars game I play gave to our family. Our kids got to see the amazing part of this extraordinary generosity, which was wonderful. People sent care packages for them and Elara, everything from head wraps to hand-made stuffed animals, restaurant gift cards, and much, much, more. One of our good friends named Barrita, who owns a fantastic chocolate shop back home, sent some funds and loving support to our family. She is helping to change the world, running a society called Sweet Smiles, which has opened multiple orphanages in Mexico. A pair of restaurant owners we know held a fundraiser where they crafted a special *Elara Burger*, and we were blown over by the response when over 10,000 dollars was raised. They came to Ronald McDonald House and personally delivered the cheque to the kids. I cannot properly express the shot in the arm these things were for us. They gave us security knowing that our expenses back home, which did not go away, were not something we needed to think about, and we could put all our focus on Elara. Unfortunately, some also came forward, showing us how nasty people can be.

One morning, we were alerted that anxiety had massively compromised the kids because a coworker wrote them a scathing message. In a condescending tone, she told our family to resist the urge to milk the community for more money. Apparently, this person saw that the original goal of the GoFundMe was 10,000 dollars but had been raised to 30,000 dollars when revealed that we needed to stay in Vancouver for an extended period of time. The organizer of that particular fundraiser was a good friend of the kids. She understood how expensive the journey was going to be, but even more prevalent, that they would benefit from being able to take some time off work should more money be raised. She was aware that even in the best-case scenario, once home again, the kids would need to heal from the emotional damage the experience brought; it would likely be quite draining for my stepson, who normally works ten hours a day, to go back to work right away.

Unfortunately, the coworker didn't see it that way and felt justified to throw some shade on a beautiful intention. That in itself was unbelievable to me. I questioned how someone, and in particular a mother, could do that.

*It's hard not to judge someone who does something like that
and not write them off as a despicable person who is as
cold-hearted as a villain in a comic book.*

Personally, I try not to care about what others who aren't in
my circle think of me. Life is too short, and my goal is to give
zero fucks about that stuff. However, it's a skill I've consciously
worked on for years, the same way I practice my approach to
confronting hard things. While hardly a perfected skill, I have
discovered that *haters gonna hate*, and there isn't anything I
can do about that. But, while going through this experience
in Vancouver, I had a tough time letting some things go. I
can't even imagine what the kids felt when this was thrown at
them. I sure know that I wanted to be Poppa Bear and tear that
person a new one.

Our family believed it was our job to rise above it. And
to our credit, we did just that. I am always so proud when
we negotiate emotional obstacles and come out stronger on
the other side. It was an exercise in mental growth, and I am
actually grateful to the person who said these awful things
because it showed me that we could overcome and move on.
Sure, it tripped us up a bit. However, within a few hours, we
were all laughing together and playing with Elara again, feeling
compassion for this person while trying to fathom the possible
reasons she would say something so toxic.

Thankfully, similar experiences to that unfortunate bit of
business were few and far between on our journey. At one point,
we received a very well-intended suggestion. A gal reached out
to me at the 11th hour, the day before Elara began her first
round of Chemo, imploring that we stop the whole thing and
try to heal our granddaughter using natural methods instead.
I understand her intention and believe in avoiding chemical

medication wherever possible. But what she may have been unaware of was that we had a world-class team of experts who have been down this path many times before with fantastic results. We learned that cancer in kids is a very different animal. For reasons beyond my limited understanding, their bodies deal with it very differently from those of adults. This is something I would never have thought of had we not gone through this experience. The good news about this is that any negativity from others through our journey was rare.

Candy and I experienced unbelievable friendship offerings from those we've known for many years—from some we barely knew, and even from people we haven't seen in decades. One gal named Paris, who I haven't seen since grade eight, reached out to me, letting me know she is now an oncologist living in Vancouver and was there for us if there was anything she could do. I remembered her very well. We had a bunch of classes together that year, and I recall her being an almost different species than the rest of us due to her brilliance. The way she studied my friends and me while we talked was like Jane Goodall studying primates; she was just on another level. She was cool too, playing tenor sax in the band while I played trombone. So, when I received her message, and she told me she became an oncologist, my literal response said through a big grin was: *Of course, she did.* Even back then, I knew she was destined for great things.

Having Paris available to text or visit here and there was invaluable. She helped me discern some of the things the doctors told us, but conversationally rather than clinically, which helped a lot. She and her family made a care package for Elara, and I am so grateful that we are still in contact to this day. Some of my close friends were massive supports as well. Richard and Shauna, the couple Candy and I spend the most time with, made sure we had gift cards to a health food store, so our groceries would be high in quality to keep our bodies strong. They arranged little escapes for Candy and me when they were in Vancouver. I went to see the comic, Bill Burr, with Richard one night and didn't feel guilty at all! God, I needed that night. Then, near the end of February, they were in town to attend a swanky corporate event down by the water in Vancouver and got to bring us as their guests. The cat ears got a lot of looks that night, let me tell ya. It was so amazing when friends like that went the extra mile to help Candy and me feel normal, even if only for a few hours. Folks back home even threw a party in our honour. In late January, a good friend who owns a sports memorabilia store called me up. He told me that he and another friend of mine who owned a restaurant in town wanted to put on a fundraiser for Candy and me. They knew we were running two houses, one at home—those bills never stopped—and one in Vancouver. They had an idea of how they could help and decided to host a dinner near the end of February. It was a private event, which they sold tickets to, complete with entertainment, silent auctions, a 50/50 raffle and more. All the food and prizes were donated, and those who put it together did so voluntarily.

It's very difficult writing about this without getting emotional. I remember being nervous about the event, thinking perhaps nobody would come, not unlike a high school student throwing a birthday party. One of my thoughts was that I hadn't heard from so many people since Elara's diagnosis who I would theoretically anticipate being there. But Jason and Matt were confident those who cared would be there, and as it turned out the evening was a massive success. Here's the thing about that: the room filled with many friends for sure, but the exact concern I had came to fruition as many people who would typically show up for a celebration, like a birthday, did not come.

However, remarkably, the room filled, and acquaintances showed up in droves. Even more remarkable was the number of people we never met before who supported the event and, ultimately, us. One gentleman named George, who I never met before, won the 50/50—not once, but twice! Both times he donated it back to Candy and me. We learned that cancer affected his family many moons ago, and when he heard about the event on social media, he came out to support it based solely on our story. We have since become close friends, and I was given the opportunity to be there for him while going through a tribulation of his own; the satisfaction of being able to reciprocate is both unique and beautiful. Many people who reached out to Candy and me were in attendance, and it's hard to describe how grateful I am, but I know being grateful serves me immensely. I encourage anyone going through something similar to keep an eye on those who reach out because even if they aren't super close, they could turn out to be friends from unexpected places.

# V

# Faith

At various times during our stay in Vancouver, the idea that something bigger than Elara's cancer or how it affected our family was growing in my mind. It is difficult describing this concept, other than from perspectives formed having lived on this earth for 45 years. I have a living spiritual side and a deep and unshakable faith. What or Who I have faith in is constantly evolving.

Growing up, I went to Sunday School off and on, but it wasn't like I went to the same church my whole life. I think my parents, who were not particularly religious, were eager I inherit the morals bestowed at faithful Christian Churches. But at the end of the day, they left the decision to me. Around the age of nine or so, they gave me a choice to go or not, and if I wanted to go, we would figure out how I would get there. My parents gave me rides if necessary, and they attended if I was in some sort of church play or production in support of me doing what I wanted to do.

My mom was, and still is thankfully, an incredible woman of faith, and although I'm not sure she believes in such things, I am sure she is an emotional empath—whatever that is…hey, I am pretty new to the concept. I also am pretty sure she is extremely proud that I have always been on a spiritual journey. Religion was something I felt to be very different from faith, but back then and even into my twenties, I could not articulate the difference. I mostly ended up being friends with either Christian kids or kids who had some sort of ethical code. Many of my Christian friends, probably due to the nature of the religion, invited me to kids' events, camps, and play nights at whichever church they happened to attend. I have a lot of very happy memories of those times. When I was older, I went to a youth group with one of my best friends from high school and established deeper relationships within the group. Many of the teachings clicked with me, especially the universal truths taught by most religions: *Treat others how you would like to be treated; Love one another, including adversaries; Forgive one another, ESPECIALLY your adversaries.* Basically, anything guided by love, I was in. I **LOVED** love and kindness so much back then, and I still do to this day. I also remember fears taught to me that were sometimes, inadvertently, like getting clocked with a frying pan to the face. I am very thankful to have received a moment of clarity early on that made a significant difference to me, one I've revisited many times in the past and regard to this very day.

I was thirteen or fourteen years old and was babysitting the neighbours' kids across the street one night. It was a pretty easy gig as the younger daughter went to bed right away, and just her older brother and I were up for a couple of hours. We played hockey in their garage and then watched a rented movie from the convenience store at the bottom of the hill. Once he went to bed, I had full run of the place until their parents returned. I remember loving having access to the food at these exotic houses where I babysat. I could hardly believe it when the parents would say: *Have anything you want*, and I certainly took advantage of that. New cereals or snack foods the folks had on hand that my mom would never buy me didn't have a chance—I felt like I hit the culinary jackpot. I got so much joy eating food at the houses I babysat at! The television was also a key highlight because those neighbours often had a bigger cable package than my parents did. I loved the expanded selection and variety of programming, and I usually ended up watching the late-night talk shows. But, on this particular night, none of that stuff mattered because I experienced the first crisis of faith I can recall.

It happened during a time I was struggling with the recent fear-based teaching at a youth group I attended. I didn't know it was based on fear at the time or that the well-meaning person who planned that particular lesson was heavy-handed in how they delivered the message. I couldn't communicate it as such, but I knew I was afraid.

***It may have been a fear of hell I was experiencing, but I don't think I was just afraid for my eternal hide.***

I had subscribed to the idea there was definitely a *God* and that *God is Love*. I adored that idea and still do. The fear was created with the idea that I could be eternally separated from that God if I didn't jump through the particular hoops required of me. In fact, I was really focused on that belief and terrified by the very notion that night. I became fixated on the idea all evening, especially after both kids went to bed. I wrestled with it, feeling cold and convinced there was some evil presence in the rumpus room with me as I tried to watch David Letterman on TV. Thinking about it now, I easily place myself back in that moment.

Thank goodness this isn't where the story ended that night. When the fear felt the thickest and so intense I thought I might go crazy, I cried out to God. It wasn't an *altar call* kind of cry or one used with the intention to save my skin. It was a cry for help, one asking for reassurance and God's acceptance for the way I am. It was a cry for Love with a capital L.

What happened next is something I have only ever told a couple of people. It was fast, intense, and unmistakable. I have a physical memory of a wave of heat and shivers that moved through me. It was like the pins and needles I get when my foot falls asleep, but this went through my entire body. The fascinating part is that I did not experience weakness, but the exact opposite as I was filled with a degree of reassurance I never felt before. I felt impossibly strong from the inside out. Even now, when times become dark for me, I reflect on that feeling, which continues to anchor me. I can sometimes bring it back by focusing on the memory, and I consciously tried that while editing this chapter—and there it is, waiting for me like a warm campfire.

I felt the presence of... *Something*. Something that reassured me everything was going to be okay, not just on this earth, but well beyond. This something reiterated that I was not a pond scum sinner who needs to continually grovel to earn my way into something more significant in the next life, but that I am a precious creature of love, and I am loved. Compared to what I actually experienced, my puny description cannot do the feeling justice. I was a kid, experiencing child-like faith. And as an adult, I was faced with deciding whether this was an organic chemical defence mechanism my body kicked in or a bonafide connection to another spiritual Universe, and perhaps even a temporary line to the Creator Themself. I decided as an adult that the latter is a better choice for me. My word, I am grateful I experienced that night as a teenager because I was forever changed. From a mindset of faith, anyway.

There were many times since that moment when I didn't describe it correctly. Religion got in the way a bit,  and I

46

sometimes had a holier-than-thou attitude towards those walking in their own direction. It was like I had eternal confidence, so my ego became activated from time to time. I could be condescending or try to imprint my moral code on others, which I was bulletproof confident of, not understanding they were on their own journey based on their own experiences. Thankfully, those times were few and far between. Well, I hope that is true. If anyone reading that last part knows me and would say I've hurt them with behaviours I just outlined, please, accept my sincere apology. Know that I most likely had good intentions behind my bad behaviour.

I delved deeply into the bible and other philosophic works during part of my teenage years. Later in high school, I had a sweetheart who went to a different church, so I switched to follow her. I became part of the culture there for a decade, and she and I married after graduating high school and then divorced not long after her college years while we began our careers. I have since learned that the human brain doesn't stop developing until one's mid-twenties; the part of the brain that develops near the end of that time is needed for critical thinking, supporting significant decision-making in life.

There were also some family dynamics that came into play, and that is putting it mildly. A bunch of crazy shit happened is another way to put it—events that could be written in their own book—and my brain was just not able to keep up with the struggle. I remember before getting married to my first wife, I studied a book on relationships with her and the pastor who married us. The concept of family dynamics came up in one of the chapters, and the book advocated that those dynamics can either make or break a relationship. I shrugged that idea off within the arrogance of my youth. At the time, I believed that if we loved each other, the rest of the family should not impact our marriage's success. In the end, the lesson I learned was that family can in fact be a huge factor, being either a benefit or a detriment within a relationship. I came to many realizations during that experience, and that relationship was the last one I had that included a church family. It's a good thing my faith is leagues stronger now than it was then. It has been challenged and questioned a lot, and I am delighted to write that it has rarely wavered.

Since that divorce, Candace and I, who were already close friends, became business partners and then romantic ones. Along with Candace came two of the most amazing boys I've had the pleasure of knowing, along with more spiritual learnings and even challenges. However, from my perspective, the similarities within our belief systems outweighed any differences we had. It was similar to that feeling I had when I was a kid, the deep knowing I felt that all would work out in the end. I love these boys, not just as an influential figure in their lives—whether they want me to be or not—but as a best friend. I love hanging with them. The little brother, Aussie, was a teenager in high school when I married his mom and moved in. I was there when he got his driver's license, and I watched him graduate and stood by as he figured out what his life was going to look like. He went from fixing and tuning Japanese exotic cars, a la *the fast and the furious*, to becoming a fantastic photographer, videographer, and digital business marketer. Cars were his passion growing up, and he thought it made sense initially to become a mechanic. However, he discovered he would rather shoot the cars on a digital canvas when they are perfect than fix them, which makes total sense to me. He has an incredible eye and a real gift for video, and I am grateful for the projects he and I work together on.

Elara's dad, Nico, is one of my best friends on the planet.

We easily ask each other's advice as we both possess a variety of knowledge and an assortment of skills that complement one another, making for a good team. We've been going to movies, working out, and generally having good times together since he was 16, long before Candace and I were even a couple. I cannot think of anything more special than adding the unique relationship of stepfather to the mix, and even though I don't use the *S* word very much, no one can take that honour away from me. Most importantly, I always wanted to be a friend to these boys, first and foremost and no matter what.

They couldn't be more different from one another, each having unique beauty and depth. Having both brought wives to our table and going back to the family dynamics I spoke of earlier, I intentionally do not want to add family dysfunction to their relationships if I can help it—I am more successful sometimes than others. We each have strong personalities, and I adore it when we do a good job accepting our differences. I am grateful they forgive me for not being perfect, and faith continues to fuel my vision that we will always be okay.

*I have always known that we would be alright in the end,*
*no matter what we went through.*
*Never has this unshakable faith been questioned ...*
*until Elara got sick.*

Until that moment, my faith was never shaken to that degree, and since returning home, I continue to work on building that faith back up again. Writing this book and doing so for a greater cause is one way I am doing so.

Even though my confidence was mostly destroyed on Elara's surgery day, it also had faith-building elements woven into it. That day was definitely the biggest test of my faith within the entire experience. But even on that day, there were people who would not allow my faith to be destroyed. Elara's oncologist, whom we will call Dr. C.—she is not a fan of pomp and circumstance—helped rebuild my faith, not just that day, but from the moment we met. She is one of the most impressive human beings I have ever encountered in my years on this planet. She's brilliant, clear, matter of fact, and empathetic, but not in a huggy way. And she is *IN FUCKING CHARGE!* I am not intimidated by many humans, and I have met many of my heroes in the athletic, music, entertainment, and business worlds without being nervous during those encounters, but Dr. C. makes me nervous. When this incredible woman speaks, I am so fascinated by her brilliance that I want to ask her hundreds of questions. I have to really, really try to shut the fuck up and listen. Someone should make a statue of this incredible individual. From the moment I met her, I began feeling the return of my wavering faith. She sat us all down for a proper meeting and let us know the exact options available for Elara. She pulled no punches while simultaneously filling me with acceptance and hope with her honesty and how she delivered it. What a damn skill set!

After talking about the procedural logistics, she looked at us as a family and said: *You are now part of a club. You didn't ask to be, but now we are in the club together.* Once she established this club status, she moved on to share who was on Elara's medical team and described how they would follow her for the next couple of decades. At that moment, I found gratefulness knowing there was someone there to lead me when I needed leadership the most. A damn fine skillset indeed!

I remember she turned, looked right at me, and said:

*There is a higher purpose for this; we don't know what it is, but it's there, and we are also a part of it.*

This may not be her exact quote, but it was the spirit with which she said it and how it penetrated my soul with the nourishment I needed at that time. I felt some resurgence of faith, a few drops of water in the desert. From that day on, whether she knows it or not, Dr. C. was a major force in keeping my faith intact, rebuilding it from rock bottom.

And then there was Elara, always the light in the room, even on the day of her surgery. Her strong energy, combined with that special super-power glow she has, supported the rebuilding of my faith even further. I watched Candy cook buckwheat water and bone broth, among many other things, lovingly and carefully, mapping Elara's eating plan to support her immune system. Every action, small and large, sparked a further resurgence of my faith.

Along with Elara, our family received unbelievable care from BC Children's hospital. When I had none left, I borrowed much-needed faith and spirit from nurses like Molly and JoJo, all led by the formidable Suzanne, whom I am also in awe of. I am happy to say we were fortunate during our experience that the lowest point happened early on. Many families aren't so lucky. For us, the idea that we are a part of something bigger than ourselves has continued to grow. After Elara's surgery, a new, unexpected friend came into Candy's and my life, one who created a much bigger understanding and made us want to help her change the world.

# VI

## Empathy

Earlier, I shared a little about how different people in our lives reacted to the news about Elara's situation and what our family was going through. Some leapt forward to help us, adding dimensions and depth to our relationship, even changing it forever. Early in the journey when so many things were up in the air, one gal, Katia, messaged back and forth with me at all hours. Whether it was something task-oriented like figuring out where we were going to live—Candy and I moved six times during those four-plus months—or just being an ear to listen and be in the fire with us while going through the hard times, Katia encouraged us as a pillar of support, and she is still there for us now.

Did we know her before? Sure. We've shared a lot of laughs before many different backdrops in the past and had a lot of fun hanging out with her and her husband. But when things got serious, so did Katia. She is one of those *low flying* angels in my life. Along with others, she taught me never to predict how people will react when times get tough. It blows me away that people like her, so unabashedly and suddenly, cared for us to the degree they did. Jonica was another one of the angels who jumped from the background straight to the centre of our lives. To that point, I had only met Jonica a handful of times, and Candy hung with her only a bit more than me. But, during those encounters, I experienced so many fun and sometimes outrageous moments. The best way for me to describe Jonica is by starting with the phrase: *Life of the party*, adding a little: *Life's too short*, and a shot of: *I give zero fucks*, then finishing with: *Authentic*. She has been through a lot while raising a family, and the truth is she gives more *fucks* than most people I know. For example, from the moment she found out what we were going through, she immediately sprang into action. This was a gal who, seeing the situation for what it was and realizing she could help, didn't hesitate to do so. She messaged Candy and me for updates all the time without worrying if it was a good time or not.

At that point, Candy and I were staying at the Vancouver Airport. This is one of the memories of the ordeal we look back at and just shrug our shoulders and laugh. Why were we at the airport? Random chance and searching for a bargain. A few days after arriving in Vancouver, it became apparent we would be staying for at least a couple of weeks. Candy and I decided to bite the bullet and get a hotel, but it had to be within a few minutes' drive of BC Children's Hospital—easier said than done as there aren't many hotels in that area. We decided that instead of individually looking for hotels in a place we were geographically challenged in, we would use the internet to assist us. We used an app we have experience with that allows us to input the parameters of what we are looking for in a hotel, from quality to amenities to approximate geographic location. It then randomly generates a list of hotels with a discounted rate. The thing is, we don't know which hotel it is until we pay.

We were at dinner with Elara and the kids one night early on our journey when we pulled the trigger. Among the list of nameless hotels, one jumped out pretty clearly from the rest. Five stars? Check. Pool? Check. Valet Parking? Yup. Restaurant? Oh yeah. And a price we were willing to live with.

It wasn't cheap by any stretch, but considering New Year's was part of the time we would be there, we could swing it. We paid, and anxiously awaited the email letting us know the name of the hotel that would be our home for the next while. The email showed up and confirmed we would be staying at the Fairmont Richmond! The Fairmont! Wow. I had taken Candy to the ones in Vancouver for a little getaway on a few occasions, and they certainly were very nice. But both Candy and I scratched our heads, trying to place the one in Richmond; we just couldn't picture it.

We finished our dinner at the lovely Italian restaurant, took Elara and the kids back to RMH and put the address of our mystery accommodation in the GPS: *It must be near the airport*, my trusty Navi Ho remarked. Boy, was she right. We followed the prompts from her iPhone, and we drove deeper and deeper into Richmond toward Vancouver International Airport. As we drove to the last exit before approaching the airport, we thought: *Surely this would be the exit we take...right?* Nope. Instructions told us to keep on moving. When the electronic voice finally said we had arrived at our destination, Candy and I couldn't do much but laugh. We were literally in the valet parking of Vancouver International Airport; the hotel was inside the terminal! Unsure what to do, a valet met us at my driver's window. Clearly, we perplexed him when we told him of our ten-night stay and asked questions about where we would park. *Everyone who stays at the Fairmont parks here*, he told us. We saw the valet rates and just looked at each other and laughed with some defeat. There went our savings by going random. We were worried about finances already, but it was minimal compared to how big that worry would get during those next few weeks.

A few nights in, after Elara had her surgery and I nearly

killed the family—always remember, the trick is to go **AROUND** the berm, but more on that later—Candy and I were back in our room, which overlooked the massive terminal. We would sometimes watch the planes come and go for hours. Elara was fascinated by that. The nights she stayed with us were so exciting for her. I loved the planes too. It was easy for me to zone out, looking out those windows, imagining where all the people who were arriving were from and wondering where all those flying out were going, distracting me from my reality. One particular night was mentally crushing for me. I was claustrophobic and really uneasy. I was lonely too.

Candy was there, and I will always be grateful to have her as my partner, but we were strained —that happened a few times during out ordeal—and I was afraid how we would afford to stay down there. A few of the folks I spent time with were reaching out, and that night, both Katia and Jonica talked me off the ledge. Katia elbowed her way into my instant messages and demanded to know how I was. I opened up and let her know how I was feeling. She started checking Airbnb's for us and reassured me that things like this always get solved, and I would be able to stay down there for my family. She really helped me know that I wasn't alone. I think if I had asked for financial help, she would have instantly given it. But I wasn't at that point yet, and thankfully, it didn't get that dire. She was right. Things just fall into place, another reason to be grateful and not forget.

Right from the start, one of the most common responses we received from people was that they didn't want to bother us during such a heinous situation. I appreciate and understand where that mindset comes from, having been on the other side, but I really appreciated hearing from people. I couldn't always respond right away, but receiving a caring message took my mind off things. And when I had downtime, messages like that provided a distraction, which was extremely important because when the situation became claustrophobic, it felt good to talk to others outside of that bubble. The irony was friends of mine felt weird chatting about things we usually enjoyed talking about, like sports, Star Wars, and comic books—yes, I am a huge nerd—when I yearned for this kind of this conversation just to feel normal, even if just for a little while.

> *However, there were those who had a deeper instinct,*
> *one that pushed them to reach out a little more forcefully.*
> *They knew we were hurting and needed*
> *emotional reinforcement.*

Jonica was also one of those people. She messaged us along the way, and she and her husband, Rick, did things like send us money to have a nice meal. She was always there for us, unlike others in our usual circle who were afraid to stay in the fire. Then, one day, she sent a message, saying she was arranging for us to meet a very good friend of hers. She mentioned this friend was like her twin, which, based on our affection for Jonica, instantly made us like her even before our meeting. Her name was Gloria Cuccione,[2] and it turns out that meeting her changed my life. It changed how I dealt with our situation and helped rebuild that broken faith I struggled with early on. We had no idea who we were meeting at the Starbucks inside BC Children's Hospital or the impact she was going to have on our lives. Not really, I mean, how do you prepare to meet someone who has literally changed the world?

When I genuinely want to compliment someone, I use the

---

[2] https://www.childhoodcancerresearch.org/directors.php

phrase *force of nature* to describe them. Many in my life deserve that moniker, and I intentionally recognize and spend time with them to glean some of the wisdom and energy they have. The moment I met Gloria and looked into her eyes, I saw the fire behind them, and I knew I just met a force of nature.

Jonica was right—she and Gloria really could be twins. Their energy levels and passion from within are nearly identical, and they have both lived through life events that shaped who they are. Gloria Cuccione fought through experiences that changed her destiny forever. When we met her, we noticed how much she valued the importance of family. She sat, listening to our story, and her entire being glowed brighter when we spoke about how we were trying to be there for our family. Just like Candy and me, Gloria loves family. She and her husband lead a very stereotypical Italian family life where the family unit is more important than nearly anything. We also connected with our perspectives on faith. One other thing we had in common is that we both had a child in our family with cancer. It was then that she told us the story of her son, Michael, and the extraordinary tale that was his life. Spending only a few moments with this woman made it abundantly clear that she garners massive strength from a source beyond this world.

Michael Cuccione was a cancer survivor, and at the age of 16, passed away from respiratory complications in 2001. During his 16 years, Michael lived a vibrant life filled with more adventures of scale and scope than many living to be 100 ever would. He was an actor, singer, songwriter, boy-band star, and author. When Gloria shared things about him, it was like Michael was right there with us, even though it's been 19 years since he left this earth. He contracted Non-Hodgkin's Lymphoma at the age of nine and underwent heavy treatment and multiple surgeries. This did not stop him from living a full life. Instead, it exposed this mighty champion's strength of character to an even wider audience. After going through treatment and becoming cancer-free, he began a remarkable journey that continues to touch many lives.

He made friends wherever he went and appeared on TV shows such as Baywatch. This led to more significant projects that showcased his unique talents. Starring in a show about a boy band on MTV called 2GETHER, Michael was able to shine his amazing radiance on so many more people. As a result, he and the band members on the show actually went on the road with major acts like Brittany Spears. But he was special in ways outside that massive success. Here is a quote from the Michael Cuccoine Foundation website:

*From the beginning of Michael's personal battle, he wanted to make a difference and started to write his own songs that would give people hope and help raise funds for childhood cancer research.*
*He produced his own CD and called it "Make A Difference" and by the age of eleven years old he raised $130,000 with the sales of his CD.*
*A meeting was set up with the President at BC Children's Hospital, and when Michael sat down, he was asked, "What do you want to do with the money you have raised?" Michael said, "I want to fund the young researchers because if we don't, we won't have them in the future".*
*The President almost fell off her chair with the incredible insight.*
*This is how the Michael Cuccione Foundation began.[3]*

---

[3] https://www.childhoodcancerresearch.org/

Gloria told us Michael had an instinct that the key to finding the cure for childhood cancer was inside the children themselves. He believed that research was the key to not just treating cancer but curing it forever. With that mandate, he sounded the rallying cry, built an army of supporters, and led the charge to change the world.

Michael Cuccione was a remarkable young visionary. As Gloria, Candy, and I all got to know each other during that meeting, we discovered things that one might consider significant coincidences. A large part of the faith I spoke of earlier is that I flat out do not believe in coincidence. We discovered that Elara's Dr. C., the head of oncology for BC Children's Hospital, is also involved with the Michael Cuccione Childhood Cancer Research Program. Suzanne, our rock of a nurse clinician, was on Michael's team all those years ago. Both women already made forever marks on both Candy's and my heart, and those marks grew deeper that day.

Gloria spoke of the legacy the Foundation created since Michael's death, and it is vast. They have raised over 25 million dollars and are hyper-focused on researching cancer in children and how to treat and ultimately cure it. Later on, near the end of Elara's treatment at BC Children's Hospital, Candy and I cornered Dr. C. and let her know about our friendship with Gloria. We knew that 25 years ago, kids with Elara's condition only had about a 15 percent survival rate, so we asked her if research from the Foundation led to why our granddaughter was going to be okay. She smiled and told us there were many pieces of the puzzle, and that many people in a variety of places were working on that puzzle. However, in her opinion, the Michael Cuccione Foundation was instrumental in putting Vancouver on the international stage of researching and implementing breakthroughs in the treatment of childhood cancer. And yes, kids like Elara benefit from those achievements every day in many places. Holy cow. Candy and I knew we wanted to use this experience to help people, to turn this negative time into something positive somehow, and the moment we met Gloria we knew that she and her *Foundation* were about to become a piece of *our* puzzle.

When we shared this with Gloria, she responded wisely, telling us there was lots of time for that, but in the meantime, to focus on our family and support Elara through her treatment. Looking back, I think that was the day Candy and I decided to write this book. Over the following weeks, we met with Gloria and Domenic as friends, and they graciously allowed us to pick their brains about all sorts of things. They were so good to us while providing frank and wise advice and answering hard questions about how they felt about going through what they did. They were so open, vulnerable, and kind, and I don't know if they will ever truly know how much they helped me. They are now family.

All of this makes me think of Elara over and over. Many people asked us if this experience changed her. It's a tough question because she is so young. One of our family members refers to Elara as a *Love Bug*, and in my mind, there is no better moniker to describe Elara's disposition. She just adores love. Even now, at only three years old, love emulates from her. We have noticed that Elara seems to have a remarkable capacity for empathy. When in a public place, if she hears a baby crying, it alerts her, and she says: *Awww, baby* in a tone so sweet I cannot properly convey it.

We sometimes watch a set of educational videos with her, which revolve around an animated family, and if one of the kids in the series feels bad for any reason, she mimics them. Even if a cartoon child skins their knee, Elara wants to help them. It's kind of remarkable. Would this empathy have revealed itself had she not gone through this experience? I'm not sure. One thing about Elara is that she has been surrounded by love since the day she was born. From time to time, I have seen other kids who don't appear to receive that consistent, unconditional kind of love, and it brings sorrow to my soul. It makes me think: *What if Elara wasn't loved that way?*

> *Seeing Elara go through the things she did made such an impact on us.*
> *I cannot imagine that it hasn't affected her in some way as well.*

When Suzanne got to know us as a family and was orientating us around what things were going to be like during our time at BC Children's, she revealed that many of the oncology ward staff work there for personal reasons. It may be because a family member, or they themselves, were touched with cancer when they were a child. Ultimately, it moved them in a direction that led them to help other kids with the same condition. This makes us wonder how Elara will be impacted and what she might do for a living when she is older as a result of being a member of this club.

When I look at how it inspired Michael Cuccione, it motivates me to want to do more to help. Gloria was right, there is a lot of time to give back, and Candy and I are starting by sharing our stories for multiple reasons. Chiefly among them is that we want to provide insights to those who have a young family member going through a significant medical ordeal. We want to provide our unique perspective as the grandparents to create bridges of understanding and support. But another beautiful reason has emerged—we want to support the work of the Michael Cuccione Foundation by sharing their story to create awareness. We also provide financially to this beautiful family Foundation that has become a part of our lives, and not at all by coincidence, by offering a percentage of every book we sell and every speaking engagement Candy or I partake in.

# VII

## Horror

Mike Fischer was my grade 12 English teacher, and he sits near the top of the list of people from my childhood who left a major impact on me. That impact resonates with me to this very day. While I desperately want him to know the positive difference he made, I also worry about him reading this book because I would never want to disappoint him with my writing skills. In truth, he taught me more than English and German throughout grades 11 and 12—he taught me about life. He was the teacher who implored his students to examine their lives and find inner purpose, rather than focusing on things like the prom or the pomp and circumstance of graduation. He taught me to look for the deeper meaning that life's moments provide. I will never forget him, and he will always live in my heart.

One of the books he had us read was Joseph Conrad's *Heart of Darkness*, which is the source material used to inspire the story of Francis Ford Coppola's iconic film *Apocalypse Now*. In both the written and theatrical versions of the story, the illusive polarizing character, Kurtz, with death close at hand and upon reflecting on the things he has witnessed, cryptically utters the words: *The horror! The horror!* It's a famous moment in modern storytelling across multiple mediums and one that has stuck with me since those English classes in 1993. To be frank, back then, I never truly understood what was so powerful about that passage or why it captured so many people's imaginations because I was just a kid, really. But, after watching the ordeal Elara went through and what other kids at the hospital or Ronald McDonald House experience, I now have a much deeper understanding of *the horror* and the images that come with it.

As I mentioned earlier, that understanding began on Christmas eve, the first time Elara had an MRI at our home hospital in Kelowna. I saw the confusion on her face when the anesthesiologist tried to subdue her, and all she could do was scream. She didn't understand what was happening and kept looking back at us like she was hoping we would swoop in and save her, hold her, and make her feel safe. To say it was traumatic does not do justice to how awful I felt seeing that. It gutted my insides, and unfortunately, that was nothing compared to what I witnessed as the journey continued. Initially, I think the worst part was seeing Elara restrained against her will. Whether it was a nurse taking blood or hooking her up to an IV or a doctor examining her when she didn't want to be examined, it was traumatizing for me. Add the reactions of other family members, especially at the beginning of the journey, and it was almost too difficult to bear. I was so out of my mind that I wanted to rip out of myself. But I will say this: I see the incredible value to our culture that doctors and nurses who specialize in children's medicine have from the careful, kind bedside manner they nearly always displayed with Elara.

Not unlike watching a suspense movie over and over again, I actually became desensitized to a degree, seeing Elara go through this process. I got used to it. I feel guilty writing those words, but it's important to note that humans have biological mechanisms to cope with such things. Before going through this experience, I did not consider there would be waves of relief along the way. I think many, if not most, parents' nightmares include a child in their family going through something like this—the fear and visions that come with that nightmare are very different from the reality. Watching Elara come out of the medically induced nap that first day was every bit as relieving as the negativity associated with seeing her go under.

So, while there are waves of horror, there are also waves of joy. On that day, I saw her recover for the first time, and the nurses brought her a popsicle, which she devoured and then motioned for another. The sheer joy of seeing Elara get what she wanted at that moment made me feel so relieved. It was like taking the word *phew* and amplifying it to record levels to the complete opposite of *the horror*. In a nutshell, that was the next four months in many ways as I navigated the crushing lows of bad news or difficult procedures that eventually swung to epic highs of things going well or being successful.

I think of those who found it difficult to reach out to us while we were immersed in all of this, and I imagine fear was part of their hesitation. But like many cases in life, the fear of an unknown event is often worse than the actual event, even the truly horrific ones. I am grateful I understand this concept now, but looking back, I still cannot believe what we went through. The worst day by far was when Elara had her surgery. While I did experience things that were hard to watch before that point, surgery day was when I felt the most helpless and hopeless, although it didn't start out that way.

Throughout this journey, the doctors did an excellent job keeping us in the loop regarding what was happening during each phase. They were so confident that it was hard not to be as well. We met two surgeons, one the day of our first appointment on December 27th, and then a couple of days later, the other surgeon who operated on Elara. They all seemed so impressive and decisive that I immediately trusted them.

*Upon reflection, I realize I was also in denial.*
*I was so sure everything was going to be okay because,*
*as scared as I was,*
*I don't think I allowed myself to think otherwise.*

They went over the procedure in a meeting with the whole family. They told us they would remove the mass, which the kids named Virgil, by surgically going in both Elara's back and front. This is something they have done before on other patients with great success, and they made a point of letting us know that this was, indeed, not their first rodeo. The procedure was scheduled for December 31st. This gave us a couple of nights to spoil Elara, and we really did. We broke her out of the hospital—with Dr. C.'s permission, of course—and took her to a cool organic ice cream place near where we were staying. I look back at the pictures of her from that night and admire how present she was. Did she have some hard experiences in the past few days? Sure did. Was she focused on them at all? Nope. All she cared about was tasting each of our ice cream cones and calling the paper-mâché cow head on the wall *puppy*.

Candy and I invited Elara to stay over at our hotel one of those nights. I am eternally grateful that the kids have allowed Elara to sleep over at our house almost weekly since she was only a few weeks old. Oh, what those times have meant to me! They have provided some of my most cherished moments, and this night was no exception. Our granddaughter didn't know and didn't care what would happen in a few short days, so we played in the hotel room above Vancouver International Airport, watching the planes come in and take off. It was like we were on an adventure, and I wish I could have enjoyed each moment as it came in—to be as present as she was back then. But, for me, the surgery was always looming, like a dark cloud on the horizon, threatening rain all day long.

On the mild winter night of December 29th, we took Elara to Van Dusen Botanical Garden In Vancouver. At that time of the year, they decorate the entire estate in lights. Acres and acres of exotic plants and trees are illuminated with some of the most beautiful displays I have ever seen. Elara was in heaven. She constantly exclaimed: *Oh wow!* Seeing her beautiful face in the glowing lights is a memory I wish I could go back to and experience again. She loved it all so much: the lights, the music, the dancing. It was only a week since the night of the block party, and to me, it felt like a lifetime had passed. But not to Elara. She didn't appear to hold on to any of the trauma or the pokes and prods during those last seven days. I am certain that all these warm and fuzzy moments we shared bolstered my strength and love for her, but I think they also fed my denial. And my reckoning was at hand because time was up. Surgery day was upon us. If I had to pick a day from my life that seemed the longest and most drawn-out, I would choose that day.

We arrived early to join the kids in Elara's room on the surgical floor of BC Children's Hospital. There was definitely tension, but it wasn't unbearable by any stretch. Elara's sleeping and eating had been interrupted over the last couple of days, so she was grumpy, but she was fine. When it was time for her to head to surgery, only the kids were allowed to go to the room where the anesthesia was administered. This would become a reoccurring theme for Candy and me as grandparents are only eligible to participate in so many things. That was a hard pill to swallow because I wanted to be there every step of the way for Elara and the kids. It got easier to accept as time went by, but I never liked it.

As a collective, we agreed always to try to find some joy, so after the kids took Elara and moments before she went into surgery, they recorded a video after Elara was given her *happy drugs* and sent it to us. There we were, crowded around Candy's phone, watching a video taken two floors down from where we sat of the cutest stoned 20-month-old we had ever seen. She was in a hospital gown, looking at the camera and talking very slowly in her Star Wars alien language. She even graced us with a couple of Seth Rogan stoner giggles while holding her favourite stuffed dog, Roxy.

I will always be grateful to the kids for having the forethought to send those videos to us as we waited alone. As I watched that video in the hospital room with Candy, reality started to set in, and my denial began slipping away. What if I was looking at Elara for the last time? I now know that questions like this are mind traps and serve little value. But it got worse because that's when the helpless waiting began with the surgery to last approximately five to seven hours. It was when they came back to the room without Elara that I knew it was real.

The plan was that a surgical team member would call the nurse's station outside Elara's room to give us an update halfway through the surgery. I wish I could have just left and watched a couple of movies that day or taken a magic pill that would have put me to sleep until the time passed. But that was not to be. I needed to be sharp and on standby in case the kids needed anything as that was my role during this ordeal. Every second that went by might as well have been five minutes. I remember looking at the kids and Candy and being impressed with how well they were handling things, at least from what I could see.

I was such a mess inside. At one point, I was lying down in the middle of the floor, staring at the ceiling. The only thing that made it bearable was that I was there with my family. I often think about some of the single parents we met on our journey with Elara. They were left to fend for themselves, being the only caretaker for their critically-ill child. We were so fortunate to have each other, even though at stressful times, we were claustrophobic and unkind to one another, but I can't imagine having gone through any of it alone. From now on, if I know someone experiencing something like this, I will do my best to reach out to them, knowing what it can mean and the difference it can make.

At the four-hour mark, we finally heard from the surgical team—everything was going smoothly. By that point, I had all sorts of visions running around in my head. The one that occurred the most was the image of my baby angel on a table, her eyes closed, doctors around her, working on her insides. It was soul-crushing. I could barely go on and didn't want to. At that moment, if someone gave me the option not to exist anymore, I would have considered it. *The horror! The horror!* But then who would be there for my family when Elara awoke? Or if she didn't? That logic was of little comfort. I love my family very, very much, but that day, logic was not something I heard very well, if at all. All I heard was the blur of the dull, slow ambient noise of the hospital around me.

After seven and a half long hours, Elara's brilliant surgeon came to let us know the results. She was wearing her scrubs and cap and had removed her mask; she looked just like a surgeon in the movies. We will call her Dr. B.; she was tired but extremely optimistic. The only hiccup she encountered was a nick on Elara's bowel, which they repaired. The tumour was not attached to her organs and came out smoothly. She then showed us a picture of it. Normally that is not my bag at all; I hate watching surgery shows on TV, but I had to see the culprit who had disrupted our lives so much. It was about the size of my fist, and it looked like a human heart to me. Dr. B. was kind of fascinated with it too, and she reassured us that things went very well.

With those words, all the worry and slowness of the day immediately went away. I am not kidding! Immediately! I was literally in the worst hell I could imagine with horrible claustrophobic emotions doing their best to crush me, and suddenly, they vanished. It's so funny how my mindset changed in the blink of an eye. I didn't want to exist just hours before but hearing that news at that moment made me feel alive again... and impatient! I wanted to see her, but it was another hour or so before that could happen. Elara had to wake up and be closely monitored, and again, no grandparents allowed. Those moments were much easier to swallow once I knew she was all sewn back up. Even now, when I look at the picture, I can't believe that thing came out of our little girl.

When we were given permission, we went down to see Elara; she was conscious but very groggy and uncomfortable. Her face was considerably puffed up, and while it sucked to see her that way, any negative feeling was overridden by the gratefulness I experienced to be in the same room with her again. The relief was unlike anything I have ever felt. At that time, I didn't know that particular day would be the darkest day of the whole journey as far as Elara's health went. I didn't know that I had hit rock bottom from a fear standpoint. Even with all that was yet to come, that was the darkest day... but I didn't know it. That is a takeaway I will hopefully have forever moving forward; sometimes we don't even realize we are at the darkest point and that it's about to get better.

I am not sure that being self-aware in moments like this is even possible, but if it is, that is a skill I desperately want. If I could go back and tell that version of myself: *While it won't be easy, it won't get worse*, I am not sure I would because of the benefit that came from the experience of going through the darkness. I think that is where the disconnect comes from when others say to me: *I could never go through a situation like that* because I truly believe they could if they had to. Although it was excruciatingly difficult, I rolled with it, taking it one step at a time as things unfolded. And yet, I look back at the ordeal as I write these words, and part of me can't believe I went through that…what a mind-fuck!

***It wasn't sudden, like a car accident.***
***If I had walked around the corner and suddenly saw***
***Elara like that with no context,***
***that would have been a different kind of horror.***

But the benefit of having a situation like this is that there is time to let things sink in. So, in the hours and days that followed, whereby we rallied around Elara to help her recover from her surgery, my initial outside perspective evolved into an inner personal level of comfort. Did seeing the impossibly small tubes coming out of her suck? Sure. But that was expected, and the X-Factor was seeing her smile or ask for a popsicle and being able to cuddle her if she cried. Before any of this happened, these were not things I would have considered had someone presented me with the idea that my precious granddaughter was going to have this procedure. However, during this process, I experienced my imagination filling in blanks in ways that were unhealthy. I learned that staying present and dealing with each thing as it comes up is a skill, and I was rapidly getting the hang of it.

The next few days after her surgery, we focused on just keeping Elara as happy as possible while she recovered. By the next day, her puffiness was already significantly reduced, and she was more herself, which included not wanting to be attached to anything and walking around. I feared she would try to rip out the tubes and lines, but she never did. When we asked her amazing medical team how babies sit still and stay attached to machines, the answer was: *They just get used to it.* It was remarkable to see that they accept and adapt. The same was true for me, although I only realized that upon reflection; like so many other things in life, the fear of what may happen can be worse than the actual events that occur. It was fear that almost caused me to get the entire family into a major car accident a few days after Elara's surgery. That was the day we found out Virgil was cancerous.

I consider myself lucky to have an optimistic viewpoint when it comes to life. When bad things happen or things don't go my way or as planned, for some reason, my instinct is to look at the bright side, and usually pretty quickly—to the point that some people get annoyed by it. My life motto is: *Average people focus on the problem; Champions focus on the solution,* and I always try to focus on that when things in life get hairy. While the vast majority of the time, that tendency has served me in dealing with negative situations, there are a small handful of instances when being optimistic has come back to bite me; it's usually when a harsh dose of reality was revealed.

Right up to the point when Dr. C. let us know Elara's unwelcome guest was cancerous, I thought it was just a cyst. The hope I had was so strong. But that hope was not to be realized, when a few days after her surgery, the medical team gave us the news. I only remember waves of that meeting. I know I was uncharacteristically quiet when I found out Elara needed two to four rounds of chemotherapy, and we were required to stay in Vancouver the entire winter and would be lucky to be home by April. They also told us that, while the surgery went well—very well—they wanted to eradicate any cells that might remain. They were optimistic. Are you kidding me? She has cancer, and they are optimistic? Mentally, I couldn't meet them there that day. My brain exploded with all kinds of thoughts: *Will the Chemo do long-term damage to our precious girl? How can we possibly do this? How can we afford the costs of staying down here?* Thank goodness there was a mechanism for the kids in the form of Ronald McDonald House and Easter Seals, but where would we stay? Completely unorganized, questions assaulted me from every angle. Uncertainty surrounded me. And in my silence, I felt my reality slipping away.

I was completely distracted, but for the life of me, I could not nail down exactly why. I was in a fog, but I knew our team was on it, and I trusted them. They had a plan and a schedule, and they were rapidly readying to kick into gear and go to war for Elara. Looking back, I am so glad there were people who weren't compromised at the same time I was. God, I am grateful there are people in my life who had my back when I wasn't nearly as effective as I'm capable of being. Since then, I try to identify moments where I might be shaken or not myself and see how I rely on others' strength. It's nice to actually recognize it as these are the people I don't ever want to take for granted.

**But it still comes down to taking responsibility, and that day, I took my eye off the ball.**

After the meeting, the family, each shellshocked in their own way, went down to the car to drive to Easter Seals, where they would stay for the next week until they could return to

Ronald McDonald House. A few days before, the good people of Vancouver received a gift from mother nature in the form of a massive snowfall. That didn't bother me in the slightest because I learned to drive in the snow growing up in Kelowna. But in Vancouver, snow is extremely rare, and when it shows up, much of the city shuts down. I believe that served our family that day.

When I pulled the SUV to the loading area at BC Children's Hospital late that afternoon, the best way to describe my demeanour was *zombie-like*. I could see, walk, and carry things, but my mind wasn't there... not at all. I cannot recall a time where I was that far away from myself. The vehicle was quiet as we drove to Easter Seals. I was on a street with three lanes, and I needed to make a left onto another three-lane street to get the kids back home. But I was in a cloud that was floating somewhere else. I saw the advance light turn green and proceeded to make the left turn, but I didn't take into account that I was crossing three lanes of traffic. I shorted the left-hand turn and ended up directly into the oncoming turning lane. It bordered a berm, and I mistook it for a snow-covered sidewalk.

Candy screamed. Back to reality, Mike! Thank goodness my Navi-Ho had the peace of mind to know what to do and ordered me to climb onto the berm and drive across it, avoiding the headlights coming right for us. Suddenly, I was awake and present, feeling a little like Han Solo as he realized he was flying directly into the path of two Imperial Star Destroyers. We needed evasive action, and **RIGHT NOW**. I hopped the small SUV up onto the white-covered partition, not knowing what was under the snow and drove across it to the other lane. Gratefully, there was no traffic in that lane. Humiliated, I dropped the kids off at the entrance to Easter Seals, where

Elara, oblivious as to what happened not two minutes before, gave me a sweet goodbye. That moment nearly crushed me.

Finding out that news and given I was so compromised, I probably shouldn't have been behind the wheel. Thank goodness nothing worse happened. As with everything on our journey, perspective kept showing up as time went on. We even turned that particular moment into a reoccurring joke over the next few months. Sometimes, when we went through that same intersection, I would say: *Hey, remember when I almost killed the family? Or, You see, everyone, the trick is to go* **AROUND** *the berm!* Thankfully, by then, comments like that would make everyone laugh. And for the rest of our stay in Vancouver, once the snow melted, that grassy berm separating six lanes of traffic had our tire tracks running across it, always reminding me to keep my focus.

I learned a valuable lesson that day. I am now aware that when I become compromised, I need to know my limits and be okay with asking for help. The journey got easier after that week, and as I complete this difficult retelling, I want to share one more awakening, which might be redundant but worth mentioning anyway. It **IS** possible to have a realization, a moment—not unlike that of Colonel Kurtz—where we are faced with: *The horror! The horror!* While it may seem like an impossible situation with no way out, I learned that even the most horrible of life's fears can be overcome, and we are equipped with far more tools than we may realize.

# VIII

## Perspective

A few weeks into our journey, we began seeing news reports about a mysterious virus causing problems in China, and it was starting to spread to Europe. The fear was that it would soon expand its reach further to North America and the rest of the world. In my head, I immediately dismissed the news as another SARS or H1N1 situation that could easily be dealt with, and I would say, considering what our family was going through, this virus barely hit my radar. It was around that time that Elara completed her first round of chemotherapy. She was discharged to our family's care between her treatment rounds, so we had to quickly learn how to conduct ourselves around a baby with a severely compromised immune system.

We were required to stay close to the hospital, so that meant we couldn't leave Vancouver. While the kids got to stay at Ronald McDonald House, Candy and I were still house hopping, but by that point, had learned the lay of the land and found a fantastic couple with a house for rent within a ten-minute walk of BC Children's that was temporarily vacant. It was awesome—a retro, 70s style split-level house that looked like the Brady Bunch could have easily lived in. After that house vacancy ended, Candy and I spent the rest of our time in the downtown apartment of a tech founder who needed to go down to California for a few months. It was a posh, open concept, city apartment complete with a 20-foot loft for a bedroom and rooftop patio nestled within all the high rises of Vancouver. It was the kind of place Candy and I always dreamed of living in when we would visit Vancouver over the years, an urban paradise. Both the house and the apartment were kind of a dream come true for us, which, again, I would have felt guilty for at the beginning of this terrible adventure.

By this point, I realized that way of thinking did not serve me and instead found the blessings the universe was offering to provide. It even took the time to do so for us in style. Candy and I developed relationships with our landlords and weren't afraid to be vulnerable by sharing our story about why we were looking for lodging. Also, I had to explain the cat ears—how that did serve us! I spent many a morning doing yoga on that patio and many an evening writing while looking at the cityscape through the ten-foot-tall windows in which the apartment brought the urban metropolis right into the living room. Candy and I took amazing walks around the seawall, the site of the world's fair Vancouver hosted back in 1986. Those walks and that geographical placement did wonders for our relationship, which of course took some of the brunt of the past few months. But we allowed ourselves to be blessed and feel joy again. Did it suck why we were there? Of course. But was it an incredible backdrop to go through the situation? Abso-**FUCKING**-lutely. And having learned to not feel guilty about such a blessing by then, well, that was the cherry on top. Ask yourself this: If you **HAD** to go through one of your life's greatest obstacles, no matter the outcome, would you rather go through it in comfort and style or be in surroundings of misery and despair? I'll take style, thank you very much. And holy hell, I am thankful! Not only did living in these places scratch a major itch, but it also kept Candy and I thinking bigger, thinking outside of our unfortunate situation, and that was good for everyone. That apartment was such a blessing. We constantly rescued the kids from the confines of RMH and brought them over, cooking delicious meals together; this made it much easier to get through the downtime. It was a game changer and another thing to be grateful for as so many families went through difficult situations utilizing way fewer options than what we had. Candy and I went up on the rooftop balcony every night at seven. Sometimes Elara came with us, and we joined the city in cheering on all the health care workers during our stay after COVID had taken hold. I have never experienced a feeling like that. Tens of thousands in the downtown core of Vancouver came out on their balconies, clapping and cheering on the health care workers as their shift change occurred. To this day, it gives me goosebumps, remembering the sound waves of positivity bouncing between the high rises.

During the times she was discharged from the hospital, Dr. C. told us that, while we couldn't put Elara in bubble wrap, there were basic things we could do to drastically reduce the chance of complications while the medicine did its job. It was all very basic stuff, but we needed to be very intentional about how we conducted ourselves. We were advised to wash our hands a lot, especially after being in public and make a concentrated effort to ensure surfaces where we were staying were disinfected. We were mindful of avoiding overly crowded areas and made sure Elara wasn't close to anyone who was really sick. It was also a good idea to do regular laundry and keep Elara away from overly humid areas. While taking these instructions seriously, our family knew we could handle the responsibility, and Dr. C. was exceptionally good at empowering us, reiterating that simply using common sense was powerful.

As the news reports of this virus grew louder and more

urgent, of course, we began to take more notice, and by Elara's second round of Chemo, COVID-19 dominated the news and conversations around us. This whole thing created such an odd sensation within me. And in many ways, as the world descended from uncertainty to lockdown, everyone around us seemed to be given the same instructions Dr. C. gave us. Suddenly, people understood what we were going through without even knowing it. I never experienced a feeling like that before; it was entirely unique.

Up until that point, whenever Elara was admitted to BC Children's, Candy and I went to the hospital every day to give the kids a break. Elara's dad stayed with her every night and was supported by his wife. We came in the morning, bringing breakfast or another concoction Candy made for Elara to supplement the hospital food. Like before, she made things like bone broth, buckwheat water, and other nutrient-loaded foods to aid Elara's healing. After all, we are what we eat, and Candy made it her mission to get as many good things as possible into her granddaughter's little body.

When we showed up, it gave the kids time to leave and rest and recharge their batteries and then return later in the day. And it gave Candy and me a chance to spend time with Elara, talking, watching movies all cuddled together, and going for walks around the oncology ward where Elara would steal the hearts of everyone she encountered. This was how we spent our days. That was our normal when Elara was in the hospital. Each Chemo round usually lasted between five to ten days. Then we had to wait 21 days in between each round to allow things to run their course with checkups in outpatient care along the way. These three-week stints were when we had to be vigilant and responsible for keeping Elara as germ-free as possible. I cannot say enough how impressed I was with the level of attention she received while in BC Children's Hospital. The entire staff made us feel like we were special, and they cared about us and gave us the encouragement and confidence we needed to get through this. We still took her out places and gave her the best life possible, but we were very careful, using what these knowledgeable doctors and their support staff taught us.

Our son was versed in keeping her dressings clean and maintaining the line inserted in her body. Boy, was that an eye-opener—a semi-permanent tube was installed in my 18-month-old granddaughter's chest so that medication could be administered at any time. It also had to be kept clean using a process skillfully learned by our son. I, naively, remember, asking what would stop Elara from grabbing the line and yanking it out. And it was just like they said: she just got used to it. They also trained us how to deal with any complications should they arise. That astounded me, but like everything else, I got used to seeing the line in her 24/7; this was something that if described to me before any of this happened, the fear would have stopped me from thinking I could ever get used to it.

By round three of Elara's chemotherapy, we were a well-oiled machine. But COVID was drastically changing things around us. It was kind of funny how folks who hadn't reached out once to us saw pictures of Elara in various social media updates and criticized us for having her out and about due to COVID. They had zero idea we had been using extreme preventative measures for months already. Although we felt the energy of judgment within these comments, we realized we were further ahead within pandemic protocol than many, if not most, of the populous. I am grateful that, at that point, I had received so many lessons, and it was easy to brush off these behavioural bugs as understandable ignorance—well-intended lack of knowledge.

Round four presented more of a grind because it was decreed that only one parent could be in with Elara at a time, and no visitors were permitted in the hospital. But by then, I have to say we were seasoned.

***It was like the global infliction of this virus was
a final exam to a course we had been taking all semester.***

We saw people freaking out, debating about all sorts of things; Candy and I chose to tune it out and continue to diligently follow the doctor's orders. By then, my perspective changed so radically, and my priorities were so concretely in line that a fucking global pandemic didn't even phase me. As a result, I sailed through those first few months while much of the world floundered in uncertainty. This was not a result of arrogance but rather what occurs when faced with emotional survival; I took what we were taught and focused on what would make a difference and chose to let the rest go. This served me in keeping COVID in perspective, and this would never have happened otherwise. All the lessons I received came in so handy, and no matter what was going on around me, I kept my eye on the prize. Then It happened...

On a spring morning in 2020, our son, Dr. C., and Suzanne were the entourage for Elara as she strode outside through the entrance to BC Children's hospital. Her treatment was complete, and as far as her medical team was concerned, she was cured for the moment and ready to go home. Her tube had been removed, and everything went exactly as Dr. C. predicted all those months ago. Impressed as always, I looked her in the eyes and thanked her. Happiness beamed from her, and it was powerful. I wanted to engulf her in a hug, but thankfully for her, we were socially distancing because I don't think she would have appreciated that very much from me. Suzanne, however, was practically coming out of her skin, wanting to embrace us all. Normally, during such times, a ceremony is performed for kids who leave bearing such good news—a graduation of sorts. COVID shut that down, but it certainly didn't change the emotions felt at that moment.

I took the cat ears off my head and happily slid them into my pocket. Two days later, Candy and I arrived back in our home for the first time that calendar year, nearly five months since we were there last. It happened that fast and was one of the most surreal sensory experiences I have ever witnessed; I felt like Dorothy in the Wizard of Oz or Marty in the last scene of Back to the Future. My parents and our younger kids made sure our place was spotless, and our neighbours had hearts in their windows, welcoming us back. The kids went back to their home, and we unloaded our luggage in ours, which seemed a little alien to us. Our cats were totally freaked out and a little standoffish. There in our quiet, calm living room, we realized that it was over. Then, during a surreal moment, standing beside our couch, Candy and I both collapsed into each other's arms and cried together. Hard. Again, one of those unique moments as all sorts of emotions flowed out of us. That night, the universe provided another unique feeling. Sleeping in our bed was one of the most comfortable places I have ever been. It was like a warm hug that engulfed me and didn't let go. The next few days were really fucking weird. Echoes of the beginning of the ordeal kept showing up. We opened our freezer and saw the popsicles we normally wouldn't have purchased but did on Christmas Eve because she had them in the hospital the day of her MRI. The most dramatic for me was when we went into our spare bathroom and opened the shower curtain to see all the toys from the last bath Elara had at our house, the one where Candy discovered the lump. Reminders like that were everywhere. And because of COVID, leaving the house was a rare occurrence, making sure these reminders were at the forefront. The good news about that is we were more than equipped to stay in the fire and process whatever random emotions would accompany them.

## One Year Later

So, a year later, how are things for us? First, let's get the important part out of the way: Elara is amazing and healthy. She came home from her one-year checkup, having passed it with flying colours. Her whole body was scanned and analyzed, and there is no sign of cancer. All markers in her blood are normal. She is even considered non-immunocompromised. Her team at BC Children's will be with her until she is 20 or so, and they will mark her progress from time to time. The expectation is that she will go on to live a regular life. But, of course, those days, weeks, months, years, and decades are not guaranteed. As secure as we feel living the lives we do, it can all change in a heartbeat, and that is something still not lost on me.

> *"Each day is a gift."*
> *This is a well-worn phrase that has an*
> *entirely new meaning for me,*
> *and a truth that I cling to.*

Besides an exception here or there, Elara has slept over at least one night a week since we have been back. And when that happens, everything stops. Candy and I literally put everything down to focus 100 percent attention on our family's most precious member. And I do my best to say *YES* to everything the kid wants. That's Pa's job as far as I am concerned—how can it not be when I have a granddaughter who's so incredible? Her hair has come back with a vengeance, and she only seems to get cuter as the days go by. Her beautiful Star Wars alien language is translated to English a little bit more every day. She's smart as a whip and as sweet as ever. The empathy she processes at such a young age is still through the roof. When she is out and about and hears a baby cry, she still says: *Awwww, Baby*, and she runs up to kids on the playground she doesn't even know, points to herself and introduces herself as Baby El Ra while making as many friends as she can. She has continued to carry that certain magic that has shone from her since the day she was born. She randomly says: *I love you Pa* all the time. I could fill books with volumes of text telling you how special she is. My love for her and the bond we have is one of the most beautiful things I have ever experienced in this world. And make no mistake, we have a tight bond. That is another lesson I have learned—a special bond is created when going through something like this with someone. I don't think I will ever have a relationship as unique as the one I share with my granddaughter. Well, that is until I am taught a new lesson. Upon reflection, if a magic genie had come up to me with the offer of seeing Elara every single day for nearly five months, I would have instantly said YES! And even though it had massive strings attached, I now know I was given that gift. And I am grateful every single day for the time I got to spend with her; it is time that so many grandparents wish they could have with their grandchildren. Like I said earlier, sometimes blessings come like a kick to the teeth. I hope and pray I will always have an unbreakable bond with Elara, and we will always be close.

Financially we have, thankfully, been okay considering

what we have been through. Certainly, we have folks in our lives who were ravaged by COVID, and I cannot be more grateful that my financial business has weathered the storm so far. But I have to say, that business, which used to propel me like a massive fire, has found a new perspective in my life. Don't get me wrong, I still enjoy many aspects of what I currently do for a living. However, our family's experience provided me with a different vantage point about my business, one that places it squarely into a more balanced state of living. Upon reflection, it never really was until we went through this experience.

Candy and I had some reentry issues for sure. Dr. C. once told us that many families don't survive these types of epic events, and I can certainly understand why. I think we sometimes took things out on each other when we got back, but thankfully, those moments are the minority. We are strong, committed, and like two fox hole buddies that survived an epic battle. We have both embarked on other personal and professional endeavours since coming home. First off, we wrote this book—I can't wait to read her half! Writing a book may have been in the realm of possibilities for us as a *someday goal*. However, our experience taught us that time is running out, and instead of having a bunch of regrets of things we would love to do eventually and never did, we decided to put the pedal down.

When I was in Vancouver, I wrote quite a bit. I wrote all sorts of things, from journal-style musings and blogs to recounting some of the eclectic tales of adventures I've had in my life. One of them had to do with my favourite broadcaster, David Letterman. In 2015, I went to one of Dave's last shows before he retired from *The Late Show*, and I experienced a whole bunch of crazy-cool shit. So, I decided to write the story down—all 20,000 words of it—and submit it to a bunch of folks who worked for Dave or wrote books about him. This has opened many doors for me. Could they end up being professional doors? I suppose only time can tell. But if you had told me a couple of years ago that I would be friendly with so many of the folks who made one of my favourite shows or that I would have received various collectables from the show, I would have sarcastically replied: *Yeah, right!* But here we are today, and I am putting myself out there because, at the end of the day, I don't want to waste any more time.

And it's not just me putting myself out there! Candy has assembled a team of impactful people and built a men's total performance app called *He Changed It*. It's a place where men can go work on themselves. She is passionate about creating solutions to the world's problems and has started by building a digital space where men can connect, utilize life-changing resources, and help each other manage the challenges during these unprecedented times and beyond. I am involved as well as the host of *He Cast*, the official podcast of *He Changed It*.[4] I have always dreamt of hosting a podcast, and since coming home, we have produced and released over 80 episodes— during a pandemic! I am super proud of that. While we have seen many folks mentally paralyzed during COVID, we just looked at it as a small logistical challenge and went for it. I have interviewed all sorts of individuals from former NHL players to filmmakers, councillors, pro wrestlers, coaches, authors, and others, listening to their stories as they share the lessons **THEY** have learned. I even interviewed Mr. Fischer to hear and share his story, and I had a chance to tell him about the impact he made on my life. I know now that everyone has a story that teaches a deeper understanding of *something*,

---

4 https://hechangedit.com/

and sharing that knowledge can help others going through something similar.

Many of my relationships have changed since coming back from Vancouver, and I am grateful for them all. Some have deepened due to unique new criteria I have that require my relationships to be more integrity-based. However, there are other acquaintances and colleagues I have created massive boundaries with because I see their colours differently since going through what we did. And then there are those whom I needed to discard from my circle entirely because having them in my life was draining and did not serve me at all. I try to have empathy for everyone, but I am also very aware that I need to protect my mental health state as well. So, I do my best to avoid situations that would have gotten me wrapped up in drama before and ultimately didn't matter. I own very little space or emotion for drama or for those I describe as energy vampires—people who take more from me than they are willing to give. In the past, I have been treated like a doormat by this type of person, but now, I am more equipped to be aware and set boundaries. I intend to always focus on what is super important to me and my family; after all, if there is anything that Elara taught me, surviving what she did, it's what is truly important. Is life perfect? Of course not. Has it been perfect? Far from it. Am I perfect? Nope. But I can learn. I can adapt. I can get through the muck if I have to. And the empowerment I received from that knowledge is every bit as powerful as attributes of the characters in the comic books I collected from boyhood to the present.

I have all sorts of things I still want to do. I want to try my hand at standup comedy. I want to speak to rooms full of people, using this book and the lessons within to inspire people and support them through similar challenges Candy and I experienced. Our mutual goal is to raise money for the Michael Cuccione Foundation to help kids get their second chance as Elara has. That is just the tip of the iceberg of the dreams I am manifesting and taking action to make come true. A huge part of this has to do with my beautiful, magical, phenomenal granddaughter...

her brush with cancer...

and how during her healing...

**She Changed Me**

# Testimonial

*I recently watched an old episode of Chicago Hope, and Mandy Patinkin delivered a line of dialogue from David E. Kelley that came to mind as I read, She Changed Me by Mike and Candace Chisholm.*

**"That is the thing about bluntness.
It engages the strong and intimidates the weak."**

*I was not prepared for what I was going to read. Mike, who has interviewed me a few times on his podcast, asked me to read what he wrote, and I gladly agreed.*

*Mike's kindness to me has been a source of energy but also quite baffling. Where did all this kindness come from? After reading about his devotion to his granddaughter, I now feel silly about taking any of his kindness. He has given more than his share to others.*

*This book makes you want to don your own pair of cat ears—not to experience the trauma and pain that his family experienced, but to show support for someone taking the worst parts of life and turning them, if you will forgive me, on its ear.*

*Reading this book will put you right in the fire with the Chisholm family. You will follow along this heart-breaking story, but instead of being engulfed in the flames, you will be engaged and find yourself hoping that, when your time comes to deal with your next crisis, you can handle it in the same way.*

*I was shocked, moved, and mostly, definitely inspired by this amazing tale of survival, family, and kindness.*

Scott Ryan, Author
*The Last Days of Letterman*
*Moonlighting: An Oral History*
ScottRyanProductions.com

# About The Author

Mike Chisholm is a self-described pleasure-seeking middle-aged nerd born and raised in Kelowna, British Columbia, Canada and has really enjoyed the four-plus decades he has spent on this planet so far.

While he works in financial services, he always had a fierce desire to branch out into writing, broadcasting, and other projects that feed his soul.

Mike currently hosts a podcast called He Cast, which is available where most podcasts can be found. He also loves mac and cheese. A lot.

**hechangedit.com**
**shechangedit.com**

# Acknowledgements

First of all, I need to begin with an apology—I am going to forget people. So, we shall start the first Acknowledgements section of my first book with a blanket statement: If you were involved in my life at all, particularly during the timeframe in which this book was written, no matter how, please know how thankful I am for you. There is no role too small someone can play in another person's life. In fact, sometimes, it's the smallest snowballs that create a massive avalanche. Thank you for whatever you did or didn't do, said or didn't say, or whoever you were to me during this, the most difficult life situation I have ever gone through.

I want to apologize to all the folks who read this who would consider themselves a volunteer grammar police force member. I tend to write how I speak, so there are definitely some sentences, despite editorial warnings, that may not be entirely grammatically correct. They were left in because I wrote them in my voice. To those dedicated members, I thank you for your service but invite you to stand down—it was likely intentional.

This book would not be here if it were not for Diana Reyers. She is an author who Candy and I met on a community TV project we were involved with a few years back, and we've been joined at the hip ever since. Diana has built a very cool publishing empire boutique called Daring to Share™ Global in which she has written and published multiple books but has also helped shepherd people with stories into writing and self-publishing books of their own. During our time in Vancouver, she was a great emotional support to us and really encouraged Candy and me to share our story with a greater audience and lean into the writing talents we both possess, raw as they may be. Diana has literally been a literary archaeologist, finding us as lumps in the earth and meticulously brushing the dirt away to show the image underneath, which is what you hold in your hands or have displayed on your electronic device right now. She has shown us infinite fucking patience during this process which has started and restarted a couple of times; she was our coach, editor, cheerleader, therapist, and collaborator. I highly recommend checking out other publications from the Daring to Share™ Global imprint and, if ever inspired, reaching out to her at daringtoshare.com

The first round of *thank yous* goes to all medical professionals who helped Elara through her ordeal. It does not take long to make me tear up when thinking of these incredibly, selfless people. The gratefulness I feel is so powerful it could stun a team of oxen. As we are also in a pandemic at the time of this writing, I personally see that anyone in the medical profession has had a lot to deal with during these unprecedented times. I appreciate everything you are all doing to try and make this a better place. The fact that you have aimed your life at healing people is not only commendable but heroic:

Dr. C., I barely have words. I type your alias, and the tears just show up. You are a giant in this world that you are literally changing while impacting families and their little worlds at the same time. Earth is a better place because you are on it;

Suzanne, there could not be a better person to deal with the uniqueness of our family than you. Not an ounce of judgement when you see our shortcomings exposed, and you have tireless effort to be helpful;

Dr. B., you are a world-class surgeon who could be on the cover of a fashion magazine. But to me, you are the real live medical version of a female Tom Cruise in Top Gun. You are cool as all get out, and you accomplished a mission of precision so important, it saved my world;

To **EVERY SINGLE MEDICAL STAFF MEMBER** at BC Children's Hospital who had even one shift helping Elara from nurses to doctors to social workers, care aides, and orderlies, Thank you. Thank you from the bottom of my heart to the top of my brain—logically and emotionally. Every single day that I spend time with Elara, the most precious member of my family, I think of what you did for her. I am present with her more often than not, and it's because of you. Thank you for changing my life in the process of what you do as a vocation.

Thank you to Gloria and Dom Cuccione for opening up your hearts to us. You took something so personal, something that anyone would have every right to never talk about to anyone else due to the pain it causes, but instead shared it to help us. Your vulnerability and openness helped us in ways you will never understand. We look forward to paying that emotional generosity forward, and you have lifelong friends in us.

Many thanks to the community of Kelowna, who rallied around us. Candy and I have always tried to give back in all sorts of ways to the beautiful city where we were born. But when it was us in need, the community didn't hesitate to help. We were blown away and will always be so proud and feel lucky to be from what we consider the best place on the planet. To anyone who prayed for us—whatever that means to you personally—shared our family's story, contributed to us in any way, we cannot thank you enough. Thank you to the local media for getting the story out there.

During this journey, there were many people who did all sorts of things, big and small, for Candy and me:

My parents, Mike and Bonnie Chisholm and our younger kids, Austin and Savanah Isagawa, thank you for keeping our house safe, our cats fed, and making sure our life back home was secure for when we finally made it back. You all took so much time out of your lives to help support us while we did our best, supporting the kids and Elara;

Thank you Eva, Tony, and your family, as well as my brother Greg, and Rose, and all the rest of Candy's side of the family, for reaching out when you did. The family What's App group messages made us smile, sometimes when we really, really needed it.

Thank you to the following people who were also a support to us:

Richard and Shauna Lockhart, you are our best friends; you gave us gift cards, whisked us away for an evening or day or two whenever you could, and you have no idea how those hours helped us;

Karen & Mike, Jared & Bella, Devin, Pansy and Ian, Debbie and Steve, The Forry family—I won't name all of you because there are so many, and I will **DEFINITELY** forget one;

Monique and her family, Matthew and Amanda, Katia and Andre, Andrew, Karen, Marty, Brooks and Kristy, Leanne, Rick, and Jonnica, thank you;

George K, you rock.

Shannon Campbell, you used your experience to help us through ours, and I hope to continue that trend by using my experience to help others. Thank you;

Scotty Mac, thanks for the night out when I really needed it;

Thanks to Lisa and Kevin V also for the night out and all the other support;

Many thanks go to Kevin G. for coming out to visit us and Kevin J. for calling to check on us;

Jody, a.k.a, Gypsy J, thank you for providing words when we needed to hear them most;

Thanks to Alex and Cindy for all your undying love;

Thank you to Paris Ann for reaching out;

Thank you to Cayman and Lucas for everything you did for our family, from organizing the GoFundMe to your words when we needed them and all your other actions of support along the way;

Thank you to the staff of Costco who organized and sent your card to us, which I heard about but never actually ended up seeing; I appreciate all who were a part of that;

Mike Brodie, I love you and your family. Thank you for being there for me while dealing with a situation of your own;

Kim Brodie, thank you for the Baby Yoda for Elara and all the well wishes;

Kris and Norm, thank you so much for the insights you shared with us, using your story as sage advice;

To my Star Wars Galaxy of Heroes Guild, the Horde of Scoundrels, thank you so much for all your support!

Thanks to Derek Marsham for taking our minds off the situation and putting Candy to work;

Shannon Crabbe, you are the most understanding business partner Candace could ever have. The fact that you held space for us while we left you solo building *He Changed It*, waiting patiently for Candace to come back to you, is amazing. Thank you for all you are, my sweet sprint sister;

Jason and Katie, I want to tell you how grateful I am, not only for your support during our ordeal but because our relationship has deepened since we have come home;

To Tim, you and Wills are still in the deep end at the time of this writing. We got to go home, and over a year later, you are still battling at BC Children's Hospital. It's not fucking fair. The fact that you were a guide and Wills was inspirational fuel for me, yet you are still in the mess, is so frustrating I could scream and do inside all the time. **PLEASE** know how important you both are to us, and we think and pray for you guys often. The positive attitudes you both have are just brilliant.

A Special thank you to some of the folks who helped us out with our accommodations while we were in Vancouver:

To the staff and management of the Fairmont at Vancouver Airport, thank you for all you did for us. You were more than hosts, and you cared for us when alerted to your unique hotel visitors who just wouldn't leave;

To the valet company, thank you so much for the parking;

To Shap, we will never forget our stay in style in the middle of Vancouver to end our journey. We hope all your endeavours are massively successful;

Damon and Kandes Krepski, holy cow, were you ever a Godsend to us. From the basement suite to *That 70s House* to the enchiladas, time spent hanging out, and most of all, the supportive words and smiles. You will always have a special place in our hearts, and I hope our paths cross many times in the future;

Barrita and Darron Durward, words are difficult to express how special you both are to Candy and me. Thank you for everything you did for us. Sweet Smiles has a powerhouse at its helm, and Barrita, you are truly a woman of greatness;

To the Staff at Ronald McDonald House, thank you for understanding our situation as you did, not only providing a place for the kids to stay during this ordeal but doing so with such a beautiful forward face. Your facility not only provides a state of happiness through the art on its walls, but your staff is so empathetic and understanding as many of the situations contained within those walls are so incredibly difficult and sometimes impossibly sad. Thank you for the distractions, food, events—until Covid reared his ugly head—and everything you have done for my family. **EVERY** time I get Elara fries through the McDonald's drive-through, I try and donate and will the rest of my days.

To all of the folks, random strangers, clerks, servers, and curious people who commented on the cat ears I wore during our time in Vancouver and sent up positive energy, prayers or gave words of encouragement, thank you!

Crystal Flamin, thank you for being such an important part of our lives. Your encouragement to share this story here and in speaking engagements has propelled our thinking towards much larger places, and you have a special place in our hearts. You inspire when you speak, you move people to be better, and we get to call you *friend*. We are so lucky to have you in our lives.

Sarah Shakespeare, you are a powerhouse. The fact that you followed our journey so closely is something I cherish because, of all the humans I have ever encountered, you are one of the most genuine. You are a light to the world around you; thank you for shining it on us.

Scott Ryan, you wrote my favourite David Letterman book of all time, *The Last Days of Letterman*, and now you wrote a testimony for this book. I am thrilled by this. The fact that we have created a friendship since I returned home is something I am REALLY grateful for, and the story of how you became a writer made me think that I could too. You inspire me. I love our dynamic and cannot wait for us to do some sort of project together, whether Letterman or Twin Peaks-related, or something entirely different.

Thank you to Nico and Jessica for allowing us to be as close to Elara as we are. It's a privilege not every grandparent gets to experience the way that we do, and we are grateful for that privilege every day. Jessica, you were faced with something no mother should ever have to face—her beautiful daughter in mortal peril. Not only did you get through the experience and love Elara even more, but you showed the world the fierce strength you possess. Nico, you are the best father Elara could ever ask for. You have such a beautiful family, and the way you step up to be there for your wife and daughter is a blueprint for husbands and fathers everywhere, including the fact that you know you aren't perfect but rather a work in progress. The way you are a rock for your family was, and is to this day, a beautiful example of love and dedication. I am honoured to have the position in your life that I do, and I love you so much. During the easy and the hard times, that never changes. I could not be more proud of how you handled yourself through all of this. Thank you for letting your mom and me be an assist to you and your girls.

Now the easiest and hardest thank you of 'em all. It's really easy to thank my wife Candace, but to gather the reasons and examples and organize them into coherent thoughts, well, that part ain't so easy because of the vastness of the task. First off, let's get this out of the way: You have the greatest smile and laugh in the world; in fact, they light up the world. You are as beautiful inside as you are on the outside. But even deeper, Candy, you see the flawed version of me more than anyone, and yet, you still keep me around. And during this ordeal, you forgave so much, held space for even more, and were the yin to my yang the entire time. You saw things that were in my blind spots and covered for me when I needed it. When I felt the most alone in the world, I still had you. You pulled me back from the edge more than once. There were times I was strong because I had to be for you, so thank you for giving me that extra measure of incentive to be so. Thank you for who you are. Thank you for never giving up on me, on us. One of the vows included when we got married was that we promised always to be each other's *partner in mischief.* You are that and so much more. Thank you for loving the way you do and for being my wife. After learning all I did going through this ordeal, the one thing I know with all my heart is that it would have been so much harder without you holding my hand all the way through it. You are the best Mimi Elara could ever ask for and loving her with you is one of the brightest joys I have ever experienced. You will change the world the way you changed mine.

Mike Chisholm
September 2021

Elara at the block party two days before
her first visit to the hospital.
On that magical night,
we had no idea what was coming over the next few months.

Elara and Pa during a very tender moment at the hospital
just around the time she had
her first chemotherapy treatment.
Hugging is also an essential treatment during such times.

Elara back at home two months after her final
treatment and release, wearing Pa's cat ears.

Nearing the end of her treatments,
Elara and Mike taking a moment to show off
their matching shoes.

Before Elara's last round of chemotherapy,
our family took a day at the Vancouver Aquarium

# she changed me

## One Ordeal, Two Perspectives

## Candace Chisholm

# She Changed Me

---

One Ordeal, Two Perspectives

---

## Candace Chisholm

GLAMMA | TECH FOUNDER | AUTHOR

LOCAL GIRL WITH GLOBAL GOALS

Daring to Share Global

Published by Candace and Mike Chisholm
September 2021 ISBN: 9781777939205

Editor: Diana Reyers
Typeset: Greg Salisbury
Book Cover Design: Kodie Beckley & Elara Isagawa

For Elara

# Testimonial

*This is an honest reflection of two souls navigating through a journey they both never anticipated being on. Their insights are raw, emotional, and at the same time, inspiring. Their experience was transformational, and these words will help to transfer their energy forward to others.*

Dr. Paris-Ann Ingledew
Radiation Oncologist, BC Cancer, Vancouver
Founder and Chief Editor www.learnoncology.ca

# Foreword
## By Diana Reyers

Early in my quest for self-discovery, I came across a quote by Mark Twain: *If you tell the truth, you don't have to remember anything.* It spoke to me, not only because it made sense logically, but because I was curious about what *telling the truth* meant to me and what depth I was willing to share it. From a very young age, I was taught to always tell the truth—never lie.

However, over time, I recognized that the truth was not always easy to share, especially when the discomfort of horrific thoughts and events were sometimes woven through. It was quite easy to describe a pleasant event or articulate when I was happy or excited but given the challenge to express something that included emotions of sadness, anger, or frustration, it became a more difficult task. As much as I was taught never to lie, I was also eventually programmed to believe that telling uncomfortable truths created a perception of weakness. My understanding was that making others uncomfortable was an infliction to be avoided at all costs. I have since learned the impactful art of sharing my truth no matter how joyous or miserable it may be for myself or for those daring to listen to my stories. Ultimately, there is always a lesson learned and a blessing gifted to me as the storyteller, as well as the reader absorbing my truth.

This epiphany changed my life, how I show up in it, and why I use it to support others to share their stories; I humbly say that inspiring others to be, do, and share their truth is the most influential thing I have ever done. I must add that, even more than writing the chronological series of events on a piece of paper, there is nothing more impactful than someone sharing how they felt from the deepest cavern of their soul while having moved through them. That meaningful expression is what creates the bond of oneness each of us spends our lifetime yearning for. Truth, and the profound articulation of it, provides the most amplified version of the pinnacle of genuine connection that we as human beings are capable of experiencing—no matter how excruciating it may be at times.

So, why are we so averse to the discomfort of some truths and yet crave more of them? Because, deep down, we know that accepting those truths provides us with what we need to acquire the gift of self-awareness that, in turn, creates amplified wisdom. And that very wisdom is the part of life's equation that gives us the confidence to be curious about even more truths, pleasant or not—both ours and others.' By being open to sharing our reality, we permit ourselves to validate the same for those who pass through our lives. Incredibly, we find that each story we tell is reflected in someone else's but shared from a different perspective. Thus, magically, the discomfort becomes comfort. We find ourselves blessed with the staggering learnings that authentic connection provides, not necessarily because we are the same, but more likely, because we are all different.

You are about to read one story by two individuals: Mike and Candace Chisholm; husband and wife; friends, partners, lovers, parents, and grandparents to wee Elara. Neither read the other's version until it was ready to be published. Together with their family, they experienced the crushing discovery that their granddaughter was diagnosed with cancer. Instantaneously, they moved through the process of supporting her parents and their daughter through treatment and recovery—all through the implosion of Covid-19. This is as uncomfortable a story as anyone can tell, and yet, Candace and Mike do so with the level of humility that leaves you speechless, the unexpected humour that allows you to tolerate waves of emotion, and the profound gut-wrenching honesty you may want to avoid, and yet, inspires you to receive more.

Each of their perspectives is profoundly different, yet you will notice how in tune they are with one another. Their writing styles are as unique and poignant as they are, and their touching accounts are equally breathless. It doesn't matter whose you begin with but be prepared that when you flip the book over to read their co-author's account, you will be greeted with a brand-new story, along with a multitude of awakenings of your own.

I was given the gift of working with Candace and Mike, providing them with the support they needed to share their story with the world. I was thrilled to participate in this project because of their adamancy to use their story to inspire others through their struggles in life, no matter what they may be. This particular story narrates the challenges of a little girl surviving cancer, so one of the first things they told me was that they wanted to donate a portion of their book sales to the Michael Cuccione Foundation,[1] supporting cancer research for children. Their goal is for every child to experience the same outcome that Elara did.

Their story is uniquely theirs, but they will be the first to tell you that many have been through a similar situation. However, how they used their truth to support them through their ordeal sets them aside from many. They believe strongly that accepting their truth, including all the good, bad, and ugly parts, supported them to emotionally survive their ordeal. As

---

[1] https://www.childhoodcancerresearch.org/

a result, they wanted to share, not just their story, but also the chaotic ebb and flow of emotions that went along with it. Their intention is that you experience what it is like to achieve the empowering role that truth can play in your life—never did they waiver on the integrity of their authenticity throughout their storytelling.

I am so grateful for the beautiful life I have been given, and I know that Candace and Mike feel the same. As you begin reading, you will realize that their story is an example of what real life can include and that their version of love truly conquers all it throws at them. If you have moved through an ordeal of this magnitude, you may relate to their initial trauma of *Holy crap! How is this happening right now?* However, their intention is not to shock you into an *Oh, woe is me* kind of mentality, but rather, inspire you to realize that *You can get through anything presented to you.*

I know, I know, you've heard all this before, but please heed my advice and delve into this book with the optimism these brilliant authors wrote it with. I promise you will accumulate as many lessons and blessings as they did by the time you finish reading the last line—each version of this story will change you just as it did them.

# Introduction
## By Mike Chisholm

When Candace and I decided to take the advice of a few folks in our circle imploring us to write a book, we weren't sure what it would look like. Over the years, the idea had surfaced from time to time. Candy and I are eclectic both in our personalities and experiences, however, I believe the reason we never pulled the trigger on such a massive undertaking is because we didn't think we had anything worth sharing, despite the contrary opinions of said folks. However, after going through what we did during the first half of 2020, that excuse evaporated.

We now had fuel for the fire that a project such as this requires. It just became a matter of process, the result of which you are now holding in your hands, either in hard copy or on a device of some kind. That process was unique, emotional, and cathartic. One of the ways this project is unique is that not only did we, a husband and wife who have been through a war together, have a story to tell filled with lessons we learned, but we also had the gift of different perspectives of said war. So very early on with our editor Diana, the format of this book was conceived—we would both write about the lessons we learned during the biggest trial of our lives, which included our 18-month-old granddaughter and her brush with cancer. We would keep our halves of the book separate and present them that way once published, kind of a *he felt; she felt* offering, and Diana would be the only one who read what each wrote along the way.

Assuring us we were indeed onto something, she encouraged us to be open and vulnerable and not shy away from the tough parts of retelling the experience and what we went through during those months in 2020. Following her advice, we did just that right up until Candace and I completed our edited manuscripts, and they were ready to be combined and published in one volume. Only one thing remained: Candy and I needed to read each other's work for the first time. Right now, I am writing the introduction to her side of this dually written volume moments after finishing her story for the first time— literally weeks before the book is scheduled to be released.

We took an evening, poured some wine, put on our favourite music, and took spots on either side of the couch. We then read each other's stories for the first time. Talk about a unique date night! The emotions going through me right now are all over the place; reading her side of our story, I both laughed and cried. I went through the entire experience again, but this time, through a different set of eyes. I recalled conversations during the ordeal we shared with each other and discovered new things Candy felt that I had no clue about until this moment. Husbands and wives are complicated sometimes, aren't we? After reading her side of this book, I can say a few things I am certain of…

First, her side is better. This is something I knew would be the case, and it was confirmed to me by the end of her first chapter. That's ok. I have no problem being second place to Candy, my formidable wife. Reading her perspective was nothing short of radically insightful, albeit surreal, and her brilliant insights hit me right between the eyes and in the very center of my heart. I couldn't be more proud to be her life partner and now her writing partner. I am so grateful for this project, providing the opportunity for me to see her expand on things I touched on and vice-versa. As I read each of her chapters, I was reminded of things I forgot to write on my side; how our memories of certain details contradict each other, showing us how memory and perspective make us fallible and more human. Receiving gifts of wisdom within how Candy interpreted certain situations allows me to look at future puzzles that life throws at us with a similar viewpoint.

But the thing I take away most from reading Candy's side of this book is how lucky I am. I am so fortunate to have such an amazing, beautiful, funny, insightful, forgiving wife who has been a phenomenal partner through the ups and downs and thick and thin that this existence amply supplies. You are lucky in that you are about to read her words and have the opportunity to gain the insights and food for thought I just did. The title of this book is *She Changed Me,* and of course, in context, it is about our beautiful granddaughter. Personally, this is not the first time I can claim such a thing. Candace also changed me, and for the better. Not to perfection, of course—in that area, we all fall short. But I know that I want to be a better man, and Candace is an inspiration for that. You will see why as her beautiful words unfold.

Mike Chisholm
September 2021

# She Changed Me

# *I*

## *Listening to Intuition*

### Starting With Our Why

We live in some unprecedented times. I don't think I actually heard the word *manifesting* until well into my thirties— shocking I know. Until then, I think *winging it* would best describe my life's greatest plan. However, as the world grew up, so did I. In 2006, the book *The Secret* by Rhonda Byrne swept our planet and my understanding of how energy works shifted. Thoughts become words, and words become actions. It seems simple enough; however, that understanding has twisted itself in my brain at times; a brain tangled with deep facets of discernment that, unfortunately, don't always work for me. In short, I have sabotaged myself over and over again: my relationships, my projects, my conquests. I have continuously kept catastrophizing until managing to have it reach reality.

So, when I remarried, after an 18-year first marriage, and then being alone for several years, I was given a fresh look and a new opportunity to see the true workings of the law of attraction. Within life, alongside my new partner with whom I write this book, I saw how this all comes together and began understanding the mechanisms of energy. With that came new friendships and relationships with those who understood this as well, and more importantly, practiced it. I am sharing this because I have lived a beautiful life for the most part. It has been touched with complications and pain, of course. And it also included times of sorrow and loss, but I have been very blessed within the ratio of privilege versus not. My life became sweeter and sweeter, and over the last few years, while rolling into my fifties, I felt like I truly found my stride. I was no longer a servant of the *keeping up with the Jones'* club or caring what others thought at all. I was excited as I entered the land of the free and home of the brave.

However, no amount of meditation or energetic mindset could prepare me for the news that one of the people I hold most dear, one who owns real estate in my heart, one who occupies many daily thoughts, processes, and decisions, gets sick. Like really sick. Life-threatening sick. As a matter of fact, those positive thoughts, as well as years I spent building a personal development library in my home and head, felt like they all converged and conspired to work against me...in the beginning. In the beginning, it was as if I was taunted by my knowledge, being tortured by thoughts including: *How could you not know? Did you attract this? I thought you were grounded!* These were just a few that pelted my subconscious. That was in the beginning.

And then life opened a new path, one I wasn't expecting, and that I finally determined I didn't ask for. I don't think anyone does. Notwithstanding, this unexpected path ended up being one I needed to approach with a *what's next?* attitude. In the end, this proved to be the greatest gift I've been given to date. But before I landed there, reality had me navigating uncharted territories on a boat built in 1971 with oars made of cotton candy.

## Tapping Into Perception

People aren't born with pure grit. Sure, over time, the wear and tear of life provides some calloused layering of one's soul that helps to navigate tough times without completely disintegrating. It's also true that it happens faster for some than others—usually due to racial, social, or geographical inequities—and also true, it may never happen for a few. But usually, we gather and place healing moss on the wounds our soul endures through trials of life. Gratefully though, that moss lends itself to new growth and an ecosystem born from these trials and is tough-enough-to-withstand further storms.

*When one's character gets tested,*
*it provides inexplicable learnings tied to unpredictable pain.*

Many things test us: divorce, job loss, financial loss, love loss, sickness, death, and everything that may lay in between. How we handle any adversity doesn't determine our worth or value. It doesn't put us in a different class or give us license to brag. It does unwind a human and earthly quality that can surprise us and encourage hope. It can show us that as much as we're made up of similar cells and matter, our differences and outcomes are what we should celebrate. This book was created for this design. Within sharing this writing, my husband and I will take you through the exact same experience with totally different outlooks. Both are beautiful in their own right, as well as heart wrenching in their rendering. Not one is right. Not one is wrong. Each viewpoint is differentiated by gender, experience, emotion, and most likely, by hormones—differences we have learned to honour within each other. Not just because we have a romantic connection, but because we realize that diversity gives us the platform to accept each other's whole being.

Writing this book has provided insight into a new level of acceptance. As we go through our experience, which happens to be one of sickness and sorrow, we hope you can identify and heal with us, no matter what your ache. And in doing so, you will see it not just from your point of view, but when you flip this book over and read the same story from the *other side*, you will feel newfound comfort in understanding. We live in a world rich with diversity, each with a brilliant, different lens where the exposure is the same, but the perception is peculiarly different. It's not bad, not good, just different. Where we celebrate our variations and where energy, manifestations, lessons, and most importantly, blessings reveal themselves to help us sympathize, love, and respect each other for the betterment of life.

## What Started the Whole Process

Anyone who is a grandparent can probably subscribe to this theory. **IT'S FREAKING AMAZING!** Seriously, it is probably the reason we keep our kids around long enough—I kid, but you get where I am coming from. So, when we became grandparents, the world just got that much sweeter. We talk about it being *all of the love and none of the fear.* Time does that. Life does that. It removes the fear of some of the unknown because experience dictates that once we go through it, a blueprint is created of how we handled it, regardless of the outcome. We know that having lived long enough with multiple blueprints piled up, fear begins to dissipate. The basic principle is that we've seen a lot of shit.

This isn't something to take lightly. It's another reason why our brain and body are cool and why we get the opportunity for do overs in life. The mistakes we make in early years are documented in our synopsis, and when we enter a similar phase, we get to review the blueprints, study the outcome, and decide how to proceed. Something I wish I would have recognized earlier in life but use as a principle now, nonetheless.

My husband and I were fortunate enough to develop a very close bond with our first grandbaby from early on. As a matter of fact, when my daughter-in-law was in labour, I was given the extreme privilege of being present. I don't take this for granted or lightly. I know it's not a common occurrence for a mom-in-law. Funny story: when she entered the world in all her six-pound, six-ounce glory, I wailed in a way only a crazy old lady can…

**She's the leader of the free world!**

I received a look of *Settle down lady, she's just a baby* from the doctor, but we all knew she wasn't. The truth of the matter is that this precious cargo knew long before I did what was coming.

If you get a chance to see the world through the eyes of a child, you'll never cease to be amazed. The joy they find in the smallest things always leaves me with a sense of gratitude. I'm grateful to witness it because it takes me back to a simpler time when I was a kid and ironically trying to speed up the ageing process. One night, when she was 18 months, we took our baby to a light show, a block party, really. Music, hot chocolate, and laughter; all the makings of the best night ever. It was a night that goes into the memory banks and makes a deposit. It's funny when you release and let go of your stress…like really let go. Everything you experience is enhanced. Music is more melodic, chocolate is sweeter, laughter deeper, and lights brighter. I wish we could live in this world, even for scheduled moments, because it really is something. And when we came home and cuddled in for the night, I witnessed the face of an angel drifting off to sleep.

## The Finding

Do you know we are the only species that doesn't use the full potential of our intuition? Fascinating. It's not to say we don't feel things or that the hair on the back of our neck doesn't stand up, but I'm talking, **ACTING** on it—it's food for thought. There is a reason why you were given it, a reason for its existence. If you can take something from this chapter, please take this because as you read this, you'll realize the importance of your sixth sense.

Waking up after that magical night, our baby girl wasn't herself. She complained of tummy aches and was having trouble pooping. By the afternoon, it was worse, and by the evening, deep concern was setting in. This is where you need to listen. A child not pooping for a day is not necessarily cause to go to the hospital, but a moment in your gut that says something is up, is something to heed.

Her mom and dad were coming to pick her up that evening, but I struggled with keeping her happy, so I decided to put her in the bath. As I took her diaper off, my heart sank. Something was there. It was a lump below her tailbone, blue and raised. *What the fuck?* Those are the only words that satisfy the angry vomit that rose in my throat—angry only because the fear wasn't enough for some odd reason. At that moment, my body needed more than one emotion to chomp on.

Have you ever had emotion so deep that the visceral reaction takes you out at your knees? Do you physically feel it bounce around like a pinball in your body? Those are deep reactions that are special to take note of. I feel that those reactions, that, if not addressed at some point, settle into organs and glands, only to surface years later and with far worse consequences.

I remember when a friend and I were once chatting, and his son climbed up on a railing, faltering in his step. I let out a *whoosh* and looked at this young fellow's dad, who proceeded to say: *I think my balls just got sucked back up into my body.* Although I don't have balls, that's what it felt like when I suddenly experienced danger surrounding someone so valuable to me. My breath literally left my body, and I searched for when it would return. Just when I surrendered to the possibility I may never breathe again, I did. But it hurt greatly, and once I recovered, I wondered: *Where did that lump come from? Did she fall, and I didn't know it?* Oh my God, no wonder she was sad, yet still tried to be so sweet. My instinct knew something was terribly wrong, but my mind couldn't catch up quickly enough.

## Now What?

The only course of action that her mom, dad, and us could assume and one that made sense was to go to the hospital. As a woman, mom, and grandma, it's easy to get lumped into the feeling of being perceived as overly emotional. Hell, the bias sometimes tells us that we are big blubbering balls of sensitivities—*insert eyeroll here*. But here is something to bank on: that is your superpower, and don't you ever forget it.

> *That empathy and that impulse*
> *are what keeps the world in order.*

The local hospital was its typical circus, which was not bad, just the usual. However, anxiety became incessant when the ER doc came in and twisted his mouth in a surly way and said: *Hang on,* while turning around and leaving the room. He came back in with an ultrasound machine, foreshadowing trauma to come.

After a short yet excruciating long wait, a pediatrician on call came in and explained that the ultrasound showed a mass. It was inconclusive, and they asked us to return the next morning. Ummm? Somewhere between the words *mass* and *tomorrow,* my senses started to dull. My swelling brain screamed: *Give her some meds and let's go!* But, from my mouth, nothing came out except a very small: okay . Why do we do that? Why do we shrink? Something I made note to explore and challenge the next time it happens…if it dared.

The next day brought a feeling of hope with the morning light. I told myself: *She is fine. How could a kid who is that happy be sick?* I ran through every bump she's ever had and how she quickly healed from each of them. My mind was going in every direction as I reminded myself of the whites of her eyes, and I went straight back to grade nine biology when I was taught how white cells work and what it all means.

After yet another diagnostic test, we waited for the very nice doctor to inform us that the test was inconclusive once more—facepalm! How have we come so far with technology and yet still seem so primitive? I was so close to screaming: Get the thingy that shows all the things. But I didn't. Instead, I used my small voice again and said: *Okay.* Dammit…. I said that wouldn't happen again; I really need to address this soon.

And then, here it was: *Come back for an MRI tomorrow, for which she will need to be sedated.* But wait, isn't there a year-long wait here in Canada for one of those and you're getting us in tomorrow??? Oh, hello panic, my old friend. There it was again. My small voice appeared, saying: *Okay. OKAY* … this is a habit, and it's really pissing me off.

So, in the early morning of Christmas Eve on December 24th, we made the now disturbingly familiar expedition down to the local hospital for the third day in a row. You can imagine getting a pediatric anesthesiologist and an MRI team on Christmas Eve Day is equivalent to coordinating a G8 conference with all the world leaders, so we started the day with an hour and a half delay, which is equivalent to 24 hours with a toddler.

After what seemed like 17 days, but was, in fact, 85 minutes, we got to see our groggy little princess. So, so, so tiny, lying in that big hospital bed as they wheeled her to recovery. *In* recovery, I was incredibly grateful to be given the opportunity to be part of her comfort team alongside her beloved Mom and Dad. She laid in my arms as the minutes passed by, knowing I would be there for her during times of fear, anxiety, or confusion, which, it turns out, was about to be doled out and spoon fed to us by a fire hydrant.

As we laid there together in the middle of a kid's hospital room on a bed, everything I owned in my body fell asleep from sitting in the same position for so long: my arms, my legs, my ass. Maybe that's why it was no big deal for the rest of me to go numb when an unassuming nurse walked in with admitting papers. Yes, you read that right, admitting papers. And then here it came...

***Tumour ... Not sure if malignant ... Surgery ...***
***Children's Hospital ... Boxing Day.***

I am sure there were other words mixed in between, but who the *hell* cares! I got the gist of it and remembered to exhale and wish I hadn't because I didn't think I could inhale again. There was a burning pain blinding my eyes. I remember thinking: *No, you are wrong. At best, it's a cyst, and you can just remove it. Don't say tumour. Sick kids have tumours.*

And thus began a tale of experience and heartache. But through it, and truly the purpose of this book, were undeniable blessings and lessons. These are the things that make this type of moment in life bearable. They are what keep us from jumping, swallowing the pills, or driving into traffic. And here, here it is...

**Lesson:** Hard things and the journey through them take us to the next level of life to understand the undeniable fact that, although messy, life is worth living and there is nothing that cannot be overcome. I promise...even when it's not evident at first.

**Blessing:** I was given the opportunity to learn this first-hand.

# *II*

## *Adopting Perspective*

### What's Next?

These are a couple of loaded little words. In some moments, uttering them can make you cringe. Like you are somehow taunting the universe. I wasn't doing this, not in the least. I have never had that kind of *come at me bitch* attitude. I have played by the rules, I have coloured in the lines, I have crossed the t's and dotted the i's while ceremoniously trying to toe the line of acceptance and worth. So, when I said: *what's next*, I truly meant: *what is the next course of action*. However, as we continued through this and subsequent journeys, these words have literally become my favourite, only in a *let's go...what's next* ... kind of way.

I am constantly reminded that life is my teacher. I once listed the things I've overcome, which I believe to be no more than anyone else, but a bountiful list, nonetheless. It was an exercise in gratitude because not only have I endured, I have also created a life worth living.

This led me to discern and consciously lean into events to gain insight, especially when managing my responses. One of my favourite expressions quickly became: *When emotions go up, intelligence goes down*. I find this thought interesting as I reflect on past life events. The more emotionally compromised I became, the quicker the flash reactions arose, and rarely were they thought out. More often than not, they were knee-jerk responses that I later regretted. My logical brain materializes, and I start rationalizing when I remember that nothing is ever as good as it seems, OR, as bad it seems. This logic proved to be one of my greatest assets while waiting for the answers to: *What was next?* Because, despite the uncertainty, until we had all the details, until we knew the facts, and until we heard from a doctor's mouth what was going on, nothing was as good or as bad as it seemed.

Then it came: the answer to that *what was next* question, and I have to say the answer began making the situation very real. We were told we could go home on Christmas Eve and spend Christmas Day with our family. And then, we had to head to our province's Children's Hospital, four hours away from where we live. That was what was next.

Interestingly, I learned something about myself that day, which I feel many of us 40 somethings fall into.... expectations. I had a narrative of what life should look like. I realized how far we were from *real life* by desensitizing ourselves with TV and social media that depict perfect lives. I saw that I set a stage and deviating from that made the whole thing seem worse. I was ashamed of my response. As I started to grasp the seriousness of it all, I realized how badly I wanted to control the outcome of what was going on. This was the holidays dammit! This was a time that embraced perfect family get-togethers, playing games by a crackling fire, eating decadent food prepared by loving hands while watching the snow fall effortlessly to the ground. This isn't a time for sickness. This doesn't happen in perfect lives.

Even as I see those words appear across my screen, I feel humbled as they remind me once again that Elara was meant for greatness.

> ***Even here, in her darkest moments,
> my granddaughter began to teach.***

She started by showing me that life isn't about perfect moments but rather that it encompasses moments that create a perfect balance of compassion, empathy, and love. With so many across the globe experiencing life's greatest afflictions, I was taught that operating as a unit is what matters. I can plan and strategize all I want, but I also need to leave room for the things that make me human. There is an inherent importance of holding space for the imperfections that connect us to others on a deeper level. Where, even if we have convinced ourselves that we love unconditionally, when the rubber hits the road and there is a possibility of deep loss, do we still? Do we allow ourselves to open our heart, expose our chest and give freely, despite the chance of being disconsolate? Yes, we do, for this is where the real gifts lie.

Nevertheless, the brevity was becoming increasingly apparent, and despite accepting that this was no ordinary holiday, we had a job to do. Adopting a mantra of *One step, one moment at a time,* we did what they suggested. And here, a new learning took place. Uncomfortable situations are easy to avoid if we tell ourselves we can't handle them. Sometimes, we give ourselves too much leeway. For instance, if you are agoraphobic, the easiest thing to do would avoid going out. Simple. But knowing that you will miss out on a lot of living can shift that way of thinking. If you start slow and small with minute shuffles with your team's help, you can build up to a tolerable place.

My realization, I now know, is that I hate confrontation and uncomfortable situations. I turtle when it comes to pain. As a self-prescribed empath, seeing others in pain travels through me and sets my nervous system on fire. So, when family members asked to come see her that night, my inclination was to say no because *I* didn't want to *feel* all their pain as well as mine. I didn't want to *see* the hurt that all her family felt. I know it sounds selfish, but don't we all have a survival mechanism put into place to help us avoid high levels of discomfort? Yet, the learning came that my vexation was no match for her inheritance of love. Yes, it was uncomfortable, but this cognitive dissonance would have kept her from receiving all that was due—love. This is something that has become part of my fabric now. Fear of pain will no longer keep me from living and experiencing life.

## Making Sense of the Insensible

Perspective—action—is an interesting word. It's a noun, but it can also be used as an adjective or verb, depending on the application. For me, during the first few days of this experience, it was more like a weapon. As I shifted thoughts and emotions around in my head like a shyster's deceitful shell game on the street, the word *perspective* kept popping up in my head. It was like I was supposed to have it automatically, or at least know how to apply it. No one teaches this in school. We aren't taught how to maneuver through life, identifying feelings and emotions so that when the time comes, we can expertly whip out our toolbox, choose the right gizmo for the job, apply it, dust ourselves off and move on. That only comes from **EXPERIENCING** the emotion. So, the first few times—and depending on how closed off we are, many times—when we come across this, it's still like a blow to the brain. Another emotion that is like this? Grief. I had a friend eloquently put it this way one day...

*Grief is an interesting thing in my life lately.*
*Just two years ago, I lost my grandson to a tragic accident.*
*Then in November, my dad transitioned*
*and two weeks later, my husband.*
*It's in my face big-time, and I don't like it.*
*No one ever talked about grief to me growing up.*
*And it is not something friends and family really*
*sit around and discuss.*
*Yet it is a part of everyone's life at some time.*
*For me, it's like the Boogie Man.*
*It lurks in the dark, and out of nowhere,*
*it rears its ugly face.*
*I am never prepared, and the littlest thing can let it out.*
*And my behaviour surprises me;*
*I feel out of control, angry, sad, pissed off,*
*resentful, lonely, ashamed, and guilty.*
*I question everything I have ever done, and then,*
*I sometimes cry the big ugly snot nose cry, or I scream.*
*I swear, I drink too much, I feel depressed, tired ....*
*and then I'm ok again.*
*Yes, grief is a weird thing.*

*Debby Andrew*

I went through the next few days after learning about our baby's tumour, and perspective became my enemy. Thankfully, we made up later.

When tragedy strikes, one can often find themselves floating between panning and planning: *How long would we be gone? What plans have to be made while away? Who will feed our cats? Should I vacuum?* Perspective was most definitely absent from the picture!! Realistically, who gives a flying rat's ass if carpets are filled with dust or not when faced with a potential life or death situation? Well, apparently, I did. Since then, I have learned that these are the times to be gentle. Because I may not know what mechanism I will choose to lean on during trauma and times of stress: *maybe*, I will need to clean, or *maybe* I will say to hell with that. There's just no place for judgement in such situations, of myself or others.

**An Upheaval**

After much internal debate, and truthfully, insight from friends and family, we arranged our affairs for the next while. And by *next while*, I truly thought at the most, two weeks. This, I now know, is blissful ignorance of the best kind. When COVID hit, we were spoon fed information that we could digest. Lockdowns started in two-week sprints for fear that if we knew the reality of it lasting over a year, many of us would have lost it right at the start. We eased into the discomfort of something we knew nothing about. This is what helped me cope—bite-size pieces of pain. Don't be afraid of that. They are digestible. They don't hurt as much going down. They are manageable. They start you on the path to perspective.

It's a marvel: the mechanisms put into place by our body and brain. Travelling in the winter over snowy roads—hello Canada—can riddle some with fear and anxiety. It certainly can be with me. But the emotional distraction of what lay ahead ironically numbed the physical fright that I would experience in the same area. Oh, the mockery of it all. Nevertheless, I was thankful for small wins. Again, perspective.

We made small talk as we drove, and in the strangest moments, tears started rolling down our faces. We took turns leading that charge, not really knowing what triggered us and knowing that those details didn't matter. And then, miraculously, the clouds parted, and this treacherous highway became bone dry as we crossed it. The fog lifted in time for us to drive through the mountain passes, and the sun shone clear on our path—another blessing. Thankfully, the imagery was not lost on me. And it was a sign that we were being looked after and watched over. These are the moments that can give you comfort when you take the time to meditate on them. You can look and realize that it didn't happen by chance, and that is not only okay to realize but necessary.

*There are times or many times, as the case may be,*
*when I realize I'm not alone and I'm going to make it,*
*just one moment at a time.*

Arriving in Vancouver was bittersweet. This is a city we often frequent for a quick weekend getaway of fun due to its proximity to home. So, on this night, before being hammered with the unknowns of her condition, we took time for ourselves. I so appreciated we did this. In times past, when faced with uncertainty, I am known to quickly adopt a martyrdom complex. I call this *My whole life is going to shit, so I will make everything as unpleasant as I can because this is what I truly deserve*-ism. I sometimes wonder if I'm alone in this way of thinking. Truthfully, I have operated this way for years, making myself feel better for being noble within my misery. Ultimately, this does not serve anyone well, least of all me. As complex life forms, humankind has the ability to discern between pleasure and pain and can simultaneously experience them without negating or diminishing each other's importance. Most importantly, this can be done without feelings of guilt. In other words, I believe it is possible to move forward through life's precarious offerings, even the excruciating ones, and experience happy moments. That is a gift. I strongly feel this realization, and practice is paramount to piloting life with the intention to avoid the pitfalls of harming self or others.

I can proudly say we did just that this first night by slowing everything down. We took a time out from the nightmarish four days we just experienced and, while our reason for being there was never far from our minds, we stayed in the moment and leaned on each other. Thoughtful and insightful friends emailed us some money and sent a note instructing us to order dinner and a bottle of wine and take a breath on them. So, this is what we did. We went to a beautiful hotel with a big fluffy bed, ordered dinner, and took a breath. Instinctively, I knew this would be a discipline we had to adopt if we were going to make it through as unscathed as humanly possible.

Be that as it may, reality—that cold-hearted bitch—woke us early the next day. I noticed my anxiety was beginning to fill my lungs. Once again, I witnessed myself creating worst-case scenarios in my head heightened by my inability to control matters. There was nothing Mike could say to help, and conversely, the solutions he offered only intensified my negative emotions. This is a slippery slope. This line of reasoning can leave me feeling lonely and full of despair. Not to mention, it put our relationship on notice, and this was not the time for us to fracture. It worried me, but I felt there was already too much going on to deal with that inconvenience. My imagination ran wild with the *what if's*. But, despite all this, and thankfully, when we drove to pick up our kids from the airport, and we finally pulled up to the arrival gate, we were met by a happy toddler and calm parents. Baby was okay, mom and dad were okay, and we were all back together as a unit. We were all set to meet this day head on. Wow! What a colossal waste of energy I just expended!!

**Lesson:** Worry is a useless emotion that steals my peace. It invades my brain and floods my nervous system with an overabundance of hormones created for fight or flight situations. It highlights my insecurities and makes me acutely aware of my shortcomings. It is a lesson that, when learned and applied, has proven invaluable in executing decisions with minimal shrapnel. It is an exercise that, when ignored, requires a lot of time and energy to repair, unfortunately, something I needed to learn… again.

**Blessing:** Once again, I was given a chance to learn and grow from it. Not everyone gets so many.

# *III*

## *The Transaction of Knowledge*

### Change Is Only Scary Until It Becomes Your New Normal

As we drove to the BC Children's Hospital from the airport, I marvelled at how the human spirit exists. We were entering into a world chalked full of unknowns, and yet we seemed to be coming up with ways to keep the chatter lightish. Another wonderment of the human body, the central nervous system, and a complex brain. It compartmentalizes what needs addressing here and now, and then magically sends out diversions, distracting us from the real issues at hand. It is magic in that it provides elevated avoidance when needed, and dangerous in that there is usually a price to pay, and more often than not, it's your mafia-like immune system that wants compensation. But on this day, I was good with avoidance. As a matter of fact, I realized my wish was that we could just keep driving, past the hospital, past the pain, and end up anywhere but where we were heading.

We pulled into the parking lot, and I sat in awe of the monster this place had become. I have previous experience with this hospital. Almost 30 years ago, my firstborn Nico, Elara's daddy, was brought here in critical condition. He was born eight weeks early, and shortly after beginning his life in the outside world, he experienced complications our little regional hospital couldn't manage. He was loaded into an air ambulance, alone with a medical team, because there was no room for his dad or me to travel with them. I watched him get wheeled away while waiting for the strength I needed to join him. Trauma. Trauma, trauma, trauma.

I was 19 years old, with barely any experience under my belt, but in one day had accrued more love for this tiny human than I thought was even possible. It became apparent to me then, that one of the most encouraging things we've learned as a growing society is the effect that past experiences can have. Those with negative emotions and outcomes commonly get classified as having post-traumatic stress, and if untreated, this stress becomes a disorder, with manifestations stored in the body. These manifestations can translate into disease, either mental or physical. Ironically, I didn't even know what effect PTSD had on me until we reached this hospital so many years later. The sight, the sound, and the smell evoked painful memories of MY baby fighting for his life. And here, in the craziest paradigm shift, I was watching HIS baby fight for her life—a trippy experience to say the least. Like so many experiences in life, if you can take yourself out of the moment and watch it from above, it would be fascinating, dare I say, even a bit magical. Only because life never ceases to surprise and stun. If I could have pulled out of my body as it were, I would have witnessed growth happening right before my very eyes. There is a certain beauty in that.

It is helpful to strive to be aware in any life-altering situation; to stay as cognizant as possible. Take in the environment and watch for physical landmarks should you get separated and lost, and emotional guideposts to remember how it felt moving through the experience. Oftentimes, moments and memories can be the very antithesis of all you think you know. For instance, I remember feeling that the physical hospital building was a *beast*. It was clean, bright, cheerful, and busy, and it gave me the feeling of a bustling cosmopolitan—a city unto itself. But what I didn't see was the pain and anguish living behind the walls, just like any urban center. It was a puzzling enigma, only complicated by the fact that I was beyond grateful such a place existed. And yet, I felt disdain for the fact that it .... well... exists.

In cinema, it's easy to see when the story begins its arc. The music increases to a dramatic haunt with the characters slowly starting the introduction dance, and the storyline begins with an elegant reveal of the nemesis, the hero, and the happily-ever-after. It's amazing what you get conditioned to when growing up with fiction. You can move through real-life situations and feel like you have seen them before, whereby you know when the heroine slays the dragon and the eerie witch morphs back into a jaunty wizard. The caution is that life can mimic your desire for escapism. You see characters in real-life scenarios play into cautionary tales, primarily because you feel you can control the outcome. It's like a *choose your adventure* novel.

Unfortunately, life isn't as predictable as a pre-written fairy tale and can't be controlled. As we got closer to the oncology ward, I felt the pull of wanting to run away or shutting my eyes to the inevitability that I needed to face—the fact that we were in a giant, beast-like hospital, about to talk to the wicked witch and her pet dragon.

Entering the ward, we approached the longest hallway I've ever walked down, anywhere. We started the trek, taking each step closer to finding answers. After checking in at reception, we were ushered to the sweetest playroom I ever saw. The toys were thoughtful, the lights bright. There was anything available a little one would want to play with. Here is where they put you while waiting for the doctor. I also became acutely aware that this is where kids needing day treatment or blood work come to play while waiting for their turn. I can only imagine what our faces looked like as families came in one by one, clearly veterans of this place. Some kids were hooked up to IV's, some were being assisted, and some sat in wheelchairs; most were bald. As beyond exceptional and factually life-saving this facility is, on this our first day, the overwhelm felt like it would never end. Subsequently, when we later witnessed other families enter for the first time, and being veterans ourselves at that point, we formed a strange kinship as members to a club we never wanted to join in the first place. We became the *encouragers*, fulfilling a sense of purpose so concrete that I will never, ever, ever, forget the feeling.

As a result of dealing with the atrocity of childhood cancer, it occurred to me that the healthcare workers' processes and skills were somewhat Ninja-like. That is how they work there, like Ninjas of health. Finding myself there, amidst the finely tuned system the staff at the hospital had established, gave me pause and comfort. I held it close for what it was—lifesaving.

If you have ever been unfortunate enough to go through cancer or a cancer scare, you will know *the room* well enough. It's the place they take you to... talk. Talk about the diagnosis, talk about the treatment, talk about the side effects, talk about the dangers, talk about, talk about, talk about... All I can say is that, although it is the most terrifying process, knowledge is power. The knowledge that leads to action, that leads to results, is power. You cannot access that power without going through the transaction. When COVID was at its height in the first months, we became inundated with knowledge. How many cases, where they were, symptoms, transmissions, all fired through the semi-automatic machine gun of the media. We could easily shut our minds to the verity, the wicked witch as it were. But the power that came with the transmission allowed us to digest and determine our course of action to protect ourselves and our families. We have the ability to attack every obstacle this way.

*What is the knowledge? How do we apply it?*
*What is the course of action?*
*That was where we stayed in power—stalwart force.*

As the details emerged about the kind of tumour it was, where it was located, the possibilities of it being malignant, the organs that may or may not be affected, and the list went on, an overarching theme started appearing in a rainbow-like lilt. Because for every hurdle, we had a runner waiting to take the baton. For every obstacle, an answer was provided. Please don't misunderstand… this situation sucked beyond sucking. It sucked on a level of 1 to 1000, a 100,000,000,000 suck. It was hard. It was painful. It was excruciatingly riddled with anxiety and stress. And yet, in glimpses of fairy dust, were the blessings. They were what I was able to witness. They were all around and presented to pull me gently through and keep me grateful in an ungrateful setting—intrinsically beautiful.

Despite this being the biggest holiday of the year with many taking time off, we had a solid plan with major players: Dr. C., Dr. B., Suzanne, Holly, Molly, Jo Jo… and the list went on and on. This didn't go unnoticed by me as I started keeping a tally of the signs that we were in good hands… everywhere. After ingesting the medical information, our social worker, Holly, stepped onto the plate. Admittedly, I ignorantly had no idea what scope social workers operate within, having only heard a smattering of stories that were not all flattering. Well, needless to say, my eyes were opened. The details they looked after were ones we wouldn't have thought of and were carefully crafted and presented with love. In times of trouble, most mamas will tell you to look for the helpers. To the social workers of this world, thank you for helping. It made me think how often negative reports of government programs are shared and how they fail us. I have and will testify that, without the programs that we were given access to, this journey would have looked much different with lasting, even more devastating, effects. Are they perfect? No. We can all falter, but I will never again choose to believe that the bad outweighs the good—it can't possibly.

After our initial meeting, we left the hospital, feeling better than we had in days. I will never underestimate what a concrete strategy executed by an unshakable unit can do in any situation or circumstance. *Knowledge, accompanied by action, creates power.* As in any good or stressful situation, many of us, at least those of us with strong ties to European roots, know that food seems to alter the physics of pain. Right or wrong, it's just simply true. So, in staying with that theme, we dried our eyes and ate. Taking our angel to a favoured restaurant from her mama's childhood, I marvelled at the amount of pasta that one could pack into a tiny, nonetheless tumoured, body. And here again, came a whitewash of realization. In this small family-owned restaurant, this food was made with love. Food and love that I recognized my own Grandma would have approved of. Love was transferred with every goopy bite. This gave me pause because I came to understand over the years that I had an unhealthy relationship with food, unfortunately just as many women do as they succumb to societal pressures.

***Here, it took the realization of a baby, sick with who knows what, enjoying the pure delight of sustenance that food is not the enemy.***

It provides life, not just in the form of energy but also in the feeling of connection that can develop around it. This was big healing for me that I am still working on and gives me hope for my future. Thanks for the lesson, angel.

After our feast, shelter was now required. I don't usually leave much to chance when travelling, so not knowing where we were going to stay caused some anxiety. Mike stepped in to take that off my plate, taking matters into his hands and looked for accommodations. In the past, we've used many websites for hotels while seeking value. One is hotwire.com[2]—not sponsored, haha—because we like that we can get a four-star for three-star rates and not know where we are staying until after we book. It's always a surprise. Knowing that the closest area to the hospital was near the airport and wanting to be there within minutes, Mike started looking there. I'm sharing this story because, for us, it became imperative to laugh through trauma. We discovered that it becomes part of the healing process triggering the cortices and releasing hormones that dissipate the long-lasting effects of trauma. And laugh we did, because as Mike was pushing the confirm button on the booking, he proudly exclaimed: *I got us the Fairmont for an amazing deal.* The Fairmont? Near the airport? No, not near the airport... **IN** the airport.

He booked us in that massive international airport hotel for the next ten days, thinking that was how long we needed to stay. It's the hotel where people stay for one night max and only if they have an early flight the next day. **NO ONE** stays for ten days—thus, the deal. I likened it to the Tom Hanks movie, *The Terminal*, where he has to stay inside the airport for months. I'm not sure anyone else will catch the humour in

---

[2] https://www.hotwire.com

this, but as exhausted as we were, things like this are what we remember fondly. We laugh about it still. Every day, multiple times a day, we drove to the airport and back to the hospital. After three days of leaving our car with the valet and paying 50 dollars a day, because there was no other form of parking, another blessing emerged. In his kind and quiet demeanour, the parking attendant asked us why we were still staying at the hotel. He was clearly confused as to why we weren't flying out somewhere, so we explained our situation to him and how we ended up at this hotel.

The story is long, and I have so much to say, so I can't go into it all, but in the end, the parking company that was independent of the hotel waived what ended up being over 700 dollars in parking fees!! They also advocated on our behalf to the Fairmont, who then heavily discounted our bill when we inevitably had to move to a longer-term place. Who does that?! Incredible, selfless, giving people, that's who. And they are everywhere bubbling up like champagne fizz, and like champagne, they appear when you need them most.

**Lesson:** Grace is infinite. We don't have limits that run the clock. The beauty about grace is this: some moments are big, some are tiny, all are irreplaceable, and none have to be paid back.

**Blessing:** I will never again doubt that the world is full of good and that good is just waiting for me to need it.

# IV

# Can I Get An Amen?!

## Being In The Moment Of The Moment

As an adult, if you have ever gone through surgery, big or small, there is a certain level of anxiety, stress, anticipation, regret, or all of the above, and understandably. Having had my share of surgeries, I know well the feeling of going from the unknown of being put under, to the stress of recovery, to the regret of not treating my body better, to undoing the damage done. This was only outweighed by a sense of loss. Whether it was the removal or repair of an organ, there is a feeling of invasion and loss.

Witnessing the upcoming surgery of a child was an unexpected experience. The bliss of ignorance was punctuated with play and fun…for her. For us as her support, it was an excruciating exercise of patience. The shadow of the day fast approached and seemed to lurk around every memory made. And yet, for the baby, she just cared about her task at hand, be it eating a new food, experiencing a new place, or cuddling a familiar body. You see, no amount of worrying changed anything for us, and to watch no amount of worrying enter her scope was yet another session in presence. She lived for that day and insisted we did too.

On Monday afternoon, Elara was checked into her room at BC Children's Hospital. My smart cookie was catching on that these *well-meaning hospital folk* usually poked and prodded too much for her liking. To stay polite, every time one of them entered her room, she exclaimed *All done.... Allllllll done.* Almost as if to say: *No need to test me, people, I am ok and nothing to see here.* It got to the point where they walked in with their hands up, indicating they weren't going to touch her. It turns out she is quite the influencer. This got rectified later on as she became far more comfortable due to a very understanding and caring staff.

However, things were still so new and moving incredibly fast when we arrived on the eve of her surgery. The poignant piece to this was the sign we received and needed at the time. When Elara's surgeon, Dr. B., came to see us to explain the surgery, its length, and what to expect, our highly empathic baby took one look at her, walked over, and gave her a big old high five. Can I get an amen?! Just when you need confirmation that the doctor who has your baby's life in their hands is the right one, it comes. We all let out a little *whoop*.

## When 24 Hours Feels Like 24 Days

I love the construct of time, or I guess, the idea of it. It's manmade. We came up with these parameters of hours, minutes, seconds, and it's fascinating to me that we measure so much with them. *This took me X amount of hours* can be harkened like a badge. We attach a fake currency to it that the longer or shorter, depending on the circumstance, that something takes us, the more value or worth we can connect to it. However, caution is needed. As we enter into a contract of experience, the precariousness of attaching a measure of time is that, if it exceeds the allotted amount, we have instant trigger responses that all must not be well. And as each segment of *time* passes, we can litigate with, and convince ourselves that not only is all not well, but all must be catastrophic. This is a dangerous argument our brain makes on our behalf, and I implore you, and myself in the process, to gently remind yourself that catastrophizing in situations already charged with intense emotion does nothing but play Russian roulette with your nerves. **YOU** have control here. **YOU** have the ability to rationalize and realize that not all the facts have been presented, and until you hear the closing argument of the case, the best outcome is still in your favour.

So, on this day, December 31st, as a departing gift to 2019, Elara was wheeled into surgery. The image of her walking down the long hallway with her dad, swimming in her oversized gown with her long locks tucked into her scrub cap, is minted into my memory bank. The helplessness I felt was indescribable and started to convert into fear and dread. We were told that her surgery would be seven to eight hours long, and they would try their best to give us updates. This is where my sermon about time in the earlier paragraph works against you.

> *An eight-hour surgery conjures up scenes from films*
> *where exhausted staff work to save a life.*
> *The imagination wields its sorcerer position.*

Nevertheless, we proceeded to take turns pacing, drinking coffee, updating family and friends, and then repeating the cycle. They kept to their word and called down once to let us know she was doing okay. Once did not seem enough, and yet logic would dictate that I would rather her surgeon stay focused on the task at hand than placate my neurosis. Finally, seven and a half hours later, we were informed that she was out of surgery and in recovery. However, I was not prepared for what I saw when we came into the room. My bright-eyed baby was puffy and swollen. She was trying to open her eyes, but they looked so heavy. Her dad scooped up her tiny body and held her tight as if trying to transfer his energy. Her mom gently cooed and stroked her sweaty hair, and as I watched the scene unfold, I once again felt the tug of terror that I had become familiar with in past traumas. I didn't like that feeling, not one bit.

The surgeon came to chat once we were situated back in the room. They were able to get 98 percent of the tumour, she said. Going any further would have put her in danger, so 2 percent was still attached. The ovary was intact. Yay! A part of her bowel needed reconstruction, but they felt that was also successful. They needed to go in from both the front and the back, which was why she was so puffy from lying face down. Oh, God. A black feeling was now burning behind my eyes. I kept saying to myself: *Look at her. She is okay. She is going to be okay.* As I mentally re-entered the room, the surgeon was finishing up saying that the tumour would be going down to pathology for testing—the next step was recovery from this major surgery. I couldn't tell anymore if I was relieved or just more worried. My emotions were starting to mutate, and where one felt reassured, the next one jumped in to question the process. Disease is confusing. Dis-ease—no longer easy, but the opposite of.

**No One Wants to Hug a Pile of Poo**

As you read this, it's not hard to glean the love I and all of us have for this tiny human. Not unlike most of you reading this book, those consuming the words on these pages have, undoubtedly, had experiences similar to mine. Maybe not cancer. But adversity, trials, struggles, discomfort, pain, as well as undying love, joy, happiness, peace. After all, we are human, and the intimacy surrounding our humanity is the common thread of our existence.

It will come as no shock to you that when I say the word *bond*, the connection I feel with Elara, belies secular laws. In other words, it feels somewhat other-worldly. I had the extreme pleasure of watching her dad bond to my dad, his grandpa, in a way that poets would write about. My dad was a hero to him. I cherished their relationship, and as I watched my dad's influence on my son, it provided a comfort and sustainability that was easily recognizable even as a young parent. I intended to always be this way for her. However, this relationship, our relationship, was placed in jeopardy for days following her surgery. When I tell this story, I can envision the disbelief in people's eyes. This couldn't possibly happen… and yet, I have witnesses to the fact.

The day she came out of surgery, I asked to be part of the overnight crew, if for no other reason than to be near her. Also, as a team, we needed to preserve energies, so we all took turns over the coming days. It's something I highly recommend, should you find yourself in a caregiver role. Burnout is real, and as much as the guilt is as well, being a martyr helps no one and quite possibly lands you in the bed next to your loved one. So that night, I stayed. After a few hours of Nico holding her in the bed, we switched out so he could get some sleep. I laid in the bed and held her. Her temperature was high, burning in fact, which they assured us was normal as her body had just been through a war. More disconcerting was her heart rate. They were having a hard time keeping it managed; I assume another by-product of the battle. Every 20 to 30 minutes, the nurses came in to check her and take her vitals. For the most part, she didn't stir, being so exhausted and more than a little medicated. I also didn't stir because there was nothing to stir from as I couldn't shut my eyes to sleep to save my life. As I mentioned, I have years of holistic training in reflexology, meridian work, and muscle testing.

*I must have run her meridians dozens of times that night,
slowly tracing the path, willing the energy to find its level.*

By morning light, she was stabilizing more. Although
beyond grateful, I had let my nervous system track out of
control through the night. I thought of the worst scenarios and
skipped through *What If* land as if checking out real estate to
set up a permanent residence there. I could not get my mind to
stop racing. I could not get my body to stop reacting. No matter
what I did. The issue with such a reconnaissance mission is that
the intel becomes confusing, and the enemy becomes yourself
with unfortunate unwanted manifestations. My precious babe
woke up the next morning and wanted nothing to do with me.
**NOTHING!** Her support, Mimi, her partner in mischief, her
biggest cheerleader… nothing. As a matter of fact, being fully
awake, she looked at me, narrowed her charcoal eyes and yelled
for her parents. Maybe this is just a blip. Kids always want their
parents when they are sick. She just needs reassurance… right?
Nope. Believe it or not, this behaviour continued for over an
entire week, almost into two! I cried rivers of tears. I felt like a
fraud and a fake. I was supposed to help protect her, she trusted
me, and when she saw I couldn't, she outed me like a con. I
ran through this narrative for days. Although the family tried
to reassure me, no one could convince me otherwise. I let her
down, and she was done with me.

One night, I couldn't take being in the room and having
her push me away anymore, so I went into the darkest hall
of the hospital I could find and wept. I wept so hard and so
long that the thought occurred to me that I may shrivel up and
evaporate into dust, which I was okay with. I called my family
and bawled. I called my friends and wailed. In retrospect, that
is exactly what I needed. I hadn't wept since my dad passed

only two months earlier. And then, just when I had resigned myself to the fact that Elara and I were not going to continue our bond like I originally thought, a miracle happened.

It was a Thursday morning, about nine days post-op. During this time, I was trying to get a tech company off the ground, so I had a couple of calls scheduled. We would sign out a conference room when either Mike or I had any work to do, so I was sitting in this room waiting for the call to take place. I had about 30 minutes, so I decided to reach out to a friend. Jody and I hadn't known each other that long, but when we met a couple of years ago, I decided then and there she needed to be in my life. A magnetic force who showed me in the short time I knew her that people and the betterment of life were her top priorities; these are the people I look to collect in my life. I texted her, and she immediately called. We chatted for a couple of minutes, me trying to hold my composure, and then she asked: How are you holding up? Back came the torrent of water. I told her what was happening and how I had resigned myself to the fact that Elara now considered me a fake, a sham. To my surprise, Jody laughed. It was an empathetic laugh, but a laugh. *Well now,* she said: *No one wants to hug a pile of poo, Candy. And from what I am hearing, you're shitting all over yourself and that stink is getting on everything. That baby doesn't care about any of that. What she feels are your own feelings. You are so hard on yourself, blaming yourself and wallowing in shame that she doesn't even recognize you.*

## NO ONE WANTS TO HUG A PILE OF POO!!

Those words vibrated through me like a Mac truck. That's exactly what I was doing. I let every negative thought wash over me, and I was rubbing that stink onto every surface. I didn't do this. I didn't give her cancer, nor could anyone have prevented it. This was a rare tumour that grows with the baby when in the belly. No one caused this, so why was I personally taking responsibility for it? I was wearing my martyrdom like a damn cloak. I needed to make sense of a senseless thing, so like women and mothers so often do, we take it on and claim responsibility to avoid the discomfort of not knowing the reason. Someone has to, right? Wrong. This happened; it just did. Just as in the coming months of COVID-19, we learned there are many things out of our control. Don't own that shit, and for God's sake don't wear it. It stinks. And no one wants to hug you. I finished my calls and sat there for another hour. I could feel my nervous system cooling. The frontal lobe of my brain seemed to come sashaying curiously back into view as if to say: *Oh hey, back to ourself, are we?* And for the first time in those nine days, I smiled a genuine smile. It was that feeling of relief of remembering to be in the moment and taking it one moment at a time. I started to laugh, sitting in a room all by myself, which I'm sure would have had passersby concerned. But the visual of me as a poo emoji popped into my head. I still use that visual to this day when I allow my emotions to jump overboard. I think: *Who wants to hug poo? Do you?*

The true test, however, was Elara. I slowly walked back to the room, opened the door, looked at her, and gave her the biggest smile I had. Here is the miracle; she looked back at me, smiled, and asked me to pick her up—honest to God, hand over heart. Mike looked at me quizzically. I told him the story and then looked at my baby, my friend. She laid her head on my shoulder as if to say: *Welcome back Mimi.*

**Lesson:** Not everything needs to be owned. If you no longer recognize yourself, it's time to trade in your secret identity. Step back, call a friend, ask for help.

**Blessing:** I now have a new litmus test by which to measure stress, and I think it's going to save my life. It's called poo.

# V

## The Realist of Reals and The Feeliest of Feels

### Like Steel to a Magnet

I had a brilliant therapist once—okay, let's be real, I've had way more than one therapist in my life, and she said: *Stress will always find the fracture and exploit it.* I always thought that was such an interesting statement. When she told me this, I was contemplating my first marriage and how dysfunctional it had seemed to become. While I was going through it, it was like every sad song on the planet played on every radio station available. I saw happy couples gazing lovingly into each other's eyes for hours at a time. Where did all the fighting couples go? I also couldn't help but liken what I was going through to any other foreign discomfort. You can break your arm, and all of a sudden, you turn into Bambi on ice, becoming *Clumsy Mc-Clumster*, hitting your arm on every available surface. Similar to constantly stubbing a broken toe or biting a burned tongue—like steel to a magnet. Pam, my therapist, told me that it's like limestone, and as soon as you put pressure on it, it splits, clean and fast. That stuck with me for over 15 years. During the time of my divorce, the pressure came in the form of change. I was changing, and that applied pressure to the fissure in the stone. Interestingly though, sickness came in at a whole new level—sickness of someone I love…well, that was just off-the-charts pressure.

## Go Around the Berm

Mike and I have been through our share of trials. I spent two years in bed with a mystery illness that tried its best to kill me. Long story short, I was slowly losing the ability to use my left side, to the point of hospitalization for paralysis. I underwent testing for every imaginable disease, and I actually think they made some of them up just to see if we noticed. But we overcame. We have had businesses that failed, employment that turned sour, friends and family that left. We overcame. Two months before Elara's diagnosis, I lost my dad, after a long and lengthy illness, of which I spent an entire month at a time in the hospital with him. We endured. But nothing, I repeat nothing, has stretched us more than this.

For all that life throws at you, for the most part, you may feel like there is a measure of accountability or participation, hell, probably even guilt. But a sick child? How does that happen? Are you freaking kidding me?! There is no way you could do anything in your life to warrant a baby suffering… is there? That—that is what rips you apart and can keep you up at night. It's what the boogie man of your forties eats for breakfast and what brings the terror when it's dark. That is what makes you snap and takes you to a place of no control. If the stars align, you and your partner will do that on separate occasions, so you hopefully don't meet each other on the plane of vulnerability and despair. But every once in a while, the emotional lottery corporation throws you a Powerball, and you both go on the same ride together.

So, when you find yourself in the test of a lifetime, it will be wise to remember that each word, each action, each feeling you feel, is a moment. Recognizing it lives in that moment helps move the sharpest point of the sword away from vital organs. You will still feel it. You will probably still bleed. But you won't die. You will have a fighting chance to heal and make it out alive.

And so, a gruelling six days after Elara's surgery, the team came into her room and made an appointment with us in their conference area away from the rest of the ward. Away from other families. Away from anything familiar we had become attached to in the short time we had been there. Ushered in, with eyes cast downward and my heartbeat splitting my ears, we walked in.

They warned us that the strongest of families can break through something like this. But honestly, they told us that in our meeting, somewhere between *Your child has cancer* and *Are there any questions?* It wasn't necessarily as cold as that, but then again, the whole freaking thing was cold. The chairs, the table, the room, it was all cold. And as we left, we all felt a little like strangers. We didn't really have any way of knowing what the other was thinking, and maybe oddly, we didn't care.

The strangest things stood out to me the night we left the hospital after the confirmation of cancer. The room was full of doctors, but I couldn't say who they were. All were women, which I thought was interesting. *Were they mothers? Grandmothers? Did it matter?* It kind of did because *How could anyone tell me this as a mother?* was a soundtrack playing through my head. I don't remember the ride in the elevator down from the eighth floor, but I remember noticing that the security guard at the door was looking at me. Did she know what we just heard? Did she care? And as we walked out the door into the dark sky that was pissing rain—a common occurrence in Vancouver, BC.

*I thought:*
*"Yeah, that's about right, the sky is crying...*
*why wouldn't it?"*

We silently piled into the car and drove out of the parking lot, hearing nothing except the remnants of sniffles from the hard, ugly cries we just had. And then, something that I will never forget happened... my husband, my rock, my confidant, the one I go to when the answers seem distant, turned into oncoming traffic! Not on purpose, of course, but nevertheless, oncoming traffic. Somehow, I found my voice, the one that didn't seem to work upstairs in the conference room, and I yelled: **MIKE!!!**

Through the grace of God, there weren't any cars coming... yet. He stopped and looked at me, stunned as though he didn't have an answer. Somehow, I squeaked out: *Please, go over the grass* —there was a divide that separated the highway lanes— and he did. Ironically, the massive amount of rain had softened the ground so substantially that we left thick, muddy tracks with our studded tires. They were there for days, even weeks, after and became a constant reminder of that night. For weeks after, Mike said: *Remember that time I almost killed the family?* It became a sadistic type of joke, dark to match our mood of that night. It was then when I realized how this man, who always seemed to find the positive in life, who held me when my legs wouldn't support my weight, who wiped many a tear from my cheek, was broken. He was hurting as much as I was, and I felt selfish, depending on him. At that moment, I was both relieved and pissed—relieved that he was human after all and pissed that he was human after all.

**Fabric of Steel**

Since then, I have threatened to leave a couple of times. He slept on the couch a few nights, and I slept on the couch a couple—not as many as him. We've had some dark moments. These are hard things to admit, but they are true and real. I pretended they didn't exist in previous relationships because I was taught the ugly was hard to look at and impossible to love. But without these realizations, without the shadow to bump the light, you don't have the opportunity to truly believe - believe that the good will outweigh the bad or that the wound will scab and heal. It becomes difficult to believe that *happily ever after* exists, but it does. And you get to choose the happy after it all.

I realized that without the pain, I wouldn't get the opportunity to wonder:

*How in the world could I get through this without him?*
*How in the world did this man*
*who has only been married to me a whole eight years,*
*give up his life to be here?*
*How did I get a human to love me as*
*unconditionally as he does?*
*How does a man love this family*
*who isn't his blood,*
*more than his career,*
*his friends or his creature comforts?*

It is that wondering and subsequent resounding answering that can take your relationship to another level. One that isn't built on just goals and manifestation. One that goes beyond creating a comfortable life, travelling the world, and having fun. One that spins thread from shrapnel and uses it to knit a fabric that feels stronger than what was earthly possible. For me, the weave became more intricate, and within it, developed flexibility that ebbed and flowed with a movement of power. I started to feel like a new piece of armour was being developed, one that was chain link, breathable, and movable, but also as tough as a mofo. It would, at all costs, protect me from any sword strikes hitting major organs in the future.

## That Hair Tho

And so, it began. On January 10th, she underwent another surgery to insert something called a Hickman line that would administer the toxic cocktail straight into my angel. *Gah!* The thought still sends chills down my spine. Immediately, and I might add extremely efficiently, we were given the rundown of the cocktail; to this day, I still can't pronounce it. She was given baseline hearing and kidney tests to determine what damage, if any, might occur. Blip, blip, blop. That's how it felt. I'm sure this is all routine for frontliners, but my brain was trying to play catch up. This was not unlike what the entire world experienced a few short months later when our entire globe went into lockdown. Phrases and words like social distance, bubble, and flatten the curve became so ordinary. Ordinary, of course, for those who process change well. For those who don't or who experience anxiety, stress, depression, overwhelm, those changes can be a cosmic ball of panic lit up with a cocaine trail of gunpowder. **EXPLOSIVE.** I had never experienced this kind or extent of overwhelm, and it gave me a front-row seat to a lesson in patience and kindness. Thank God the experts we engaged with were both patient and kind to this overwhelmed Glamma!

If you have had the unfortunate experience of eradicating cancer out of your body or watched someone close to you experience the same, you may identify with the following: the process is gruelling, unforgiving, and cruel. It is an endless round of poison—let's call a duck a duck, shall we?—of medication, the revival of white cells, immune cells, hemoglobin, and others, and then wash, rinse, repeat. It is a four-round assault on the body, and in many, if not all cases, it is necessary for survival. However, as luck would have it, we are a family of healers and believe in complementary therapies to punctuate the treatment, including nutrition, energy, and love.

And so, we started a round-robin of organic homemade bone broths, buckwheat teas, marine phytoplankton, spirulina, and a host of other goodies. Watching her not just survive but actually thrive through her regimen was a miraculous display of what the human body can accomplish. In years gone by, through my schooling and training, I read and witnessed recovery due to the sheer inner workings of immune systems, lymphatic systems, organs, and all the connective bits.

But unfortunately, sitting in disease can often leave you soggy and wet with the unfairness of it all. I get that, and I see you. However, every day, your body fights for you until you breathe your last breath. It measures and times releases. It craves vitamins and minerals it wants to extract from food and reminds you how to get them. It puts you to sleep to recover and makes you move for clemency. So, if you hear any one word from this story, it's this…. *Listen.* Listen to what your body asks. Listen to its pleas. Listen to it. It needs you, and you need it, and together, you can do this.

In saying all that, I was incredibly encouraged by Elara's progress, as were her teams. So much so that by week three, when she still hadn't lost her beautiful locks, I felt my ego revving up; perhaps, the protocol of nutrition we had her on will support her to bypass hair loss. Maybe she will be one of the lucky ones. Perhaps this is what she will teach them; how to keep her hair. While it sounds vain to worry about such a small thing in the grand scheme of fighting for her life, the truth is that I had inserted her hair into her identity. I wouldn't have admitted that before, probably for fear of the judgement from people, thinking I was… vain. From birth, she looked like she was wearing a wig, an expensive, gorgeous wig. It's the first thing I saw when she was crowning. Everywhere we went, it was what people commented on right away—her hair. She had the hair of legendary folklore. Samson!

**I mistakenly believed it was her superpower.**
**It turns out, it was just window dressing.**

In the fourth week, when the first chestnut strands started hitting the floor, the reality of all that began setting in. Tears streamed from my eyes as I swept and held those precious threads of life. Not to be forgotten, my ego reared again, telling me I obviously hadn't tried hard enough to provide her with the nutrition she needed. Surely if I had, this hair loss would have been spared. Thank you, ego, but I don't need the extra help in the guilt department!

The next day after her nap, heaps of her hair clung to her pillow, her sheets, and her stuffed dog. It was almost like these little life rafts were lingering a little longer to something that was hers. By the third day that week, the dead hair was knotting with the remaining locks and created a very impressive, yet painful, dreadlock. It was time to shave her head. As her dad took the clippers to her, she looked up and flashed us a sporadically placed toothy grin. How was she smiling? Shouldn't she be scared? And then it dawned on me; she had no attachment to the hair. It was simply a thing that got in her eyes most days and took far too much time away from playing, having it constantly washed, blow-dried, and put up. I'm not so sure she didn't like her hair. She just didn't care if it was there or not. It didn't change the way she felt, which is happy. It didn't change the feeling she has when around her family, which is love. And it certainly didn't change the outcome of her health, which is great!

I think that by now, you have the gist of the theme of this book. For close to 50 years, I put far too much importance on *things*, backwardly prioritizing life's balance and mistakenly looking to be skinny, beautiful, rich, and successful. No one ever thinks that cancer can happen to them. No one plans for divorce, death, pandemics, natural disasters, or total loss. Well, we certainly didn't. But the offset has brought my reality to a much more fulfilling climax. I can no longer stand the nonsense that seems to float in the air so freely—drama, hate, and injustice—when challenged with crisis, seem insignificant, petty, and such a complete waste of time. Life. Is. Precious. It is the only thing that makes the 80 or, if you're lucky, 90 years on this planet worth bearing. Life and its messiness can be full of love, happiness, joy, peace, kindness, and faith. Don't believe me? I have a few friends up on the oncology ward of Children's Hospital who would love to teach you otherwise.

**Lesson:** If you are loved, happy, and have your health, the rest is just stuff. Sometimes, it's amazing stuff that makes your world easier and more enjoyable. Sometimes, it's horrible stuff that hurts and makes you wince, and for whatever reason, we sometimes wear that like a badge too. But at the end of the day, you genuinely don't need to attach yourself to any of it.

It doesn't define you. It doesn't make you better or worse. It doesn't enhance your capabilities to add to the betterment of the human race. That is just you. So, with everything stripped away, can you smile, hug, and love? I truly believe that as you go through some of life's most harrowing tribulations, you will find who you are, stripped of attachments and able to just be.

**Blessing:** I've learned that attachments are just things on your vacuum that make it easier to clean.

# VI

## We Rise Together

**Time. What. The. Hell.**

As I mentioned earlier, time is an interesting construct. Also, as I mentioned before, while the keeping of time is human-derived, the controlling of time is elusive to all humans. When waiting for answers, results, or communication, time seemingly becomes something tangible, as if you can hold it. If you are, in fact, waiting for results, time can be as physical as water, flowing, pooling, or at its worst, rising over your head. As a global unit wading through the unknown of a pandemic, the majority of us felt time melt together. Days blended into weeks, into months and morphed into a year. But in reality, remembering that the measurement of time and its parameters are simply made up became a helpful reminder. Inevitably, time will pass, but it cannot, nor will it drown me.

For the first while after having gone through the first round of chemo, and then waiting for results from blood work and a variety of other tests, our time in treatment seemed to be taken up with a *hurry and wait* system—*hurry* from one appointment to the next, then *wait* for results. But soon, the systems and routine settled into place. I'll never forget, a mere three weeks after we arrived, a new family showed up in the oncology playroom. One look at the mama and the fear set deep in her pupils, and I knew they must have just received the news. Sure enough, after a couple of gentle questions, she let us know that her ten-month-old was diagnosed with leukemia. Her mama intuition told her that the lethargy she was witnessing in her baby over Christmas wasn't normal; a few blood tests later, and here they were. My heart broke for her. And then, as I seemed to travel outside of my body, I witnessed myself, tired and haggard, giving her the lowdown of the place, where the best snacks were kept, who the best nurses were, and which toys to take to the room to quell the ever-persistent toddler boredom. It was like watching an old black and white war movie with the veteran, broken and bloodied, cigarette hanging precariously from his sunburnt lips. His pupils are dilated with the horrors of all he has witnessed thus far as he looks at the new recruit still shiny from the drop-off, his uniform still freshly pressed. As the fear begins taking shape on this newbie, the jaded veteran flicks his cigarette, side-steps a grenade, and robotically takes him by the hand to his post. The difference in their arrival to war… three weeks. Time.

However, in the ebb and flow of days that are focused on one thing—healing—you become a benefactor of observance because now you have the time. When faced with trials and are numbed by the seconds that pass ever so slowly, you get to observe…love. It shows up in the unlikeliest of places and appears without prediction. It takes on a pattern that a busy life would miss; a pattern that only the stymied observance of time can reveal.

*"Look for the helpers"*
***A war cry echoed by many a mother to their children***
***in preparation for a day of trial.***
***Time slows, helpers show.***
***Magic.***

## The Helpers

We witnessed this on an unworldly level, being bombarded by the most caring, thoughtful messages and petitions for prayers and love. More often than not, these were from people we barely knew, and sometimes, we didn't know them at all. Through the magic of social media, news travelled far and wide between communities. The extraordinary amount of support was humbling and somewhat overwhelming, with messages pouring in with offerings of what people could do. I will never forget one of my best friends, Lisa, sending *dinner money* the first night we were there, and then, she went on to coral her posse of gals to do the same. Knowing what we were carrying, our best friends, Richard and Shanuna, gave us gift cards to health stores, to ensure we materially feed and nourish our soul. My sister Holly sent us money that I know wasn't extra, and my niece Paris followed suit. They put together the most thoughtful care packages that healed my heart. Comforts from home and *extras* to heal. The love that went into these will never, ever be forgotten. My wish is that I remember to do the same when needed. And then, an amazing but new friend to me, Jonica, reached out to her network to help. In that, one of the most incredible interactions and one of the motivations to write this book ensued. We were honoured to meet Gloria Cuccione, a founding member of an incredible organization responsible for millions of dollars in research for childhood cancer and subsequent hundreds of lives saved. That organization is the Michael Cuccione Foundation[3]. Michael is Gloria's son, and he passed away from complications with childhood cancer 25 years ago. So, as this lightning bolt of

---

[3] https://www.childhoodcancerresearch.org/

inspiration comforted us, helped us, and guided us, it also set off a desire to do the same one day.

Financially, people wanted to give, and give they did. Half a dozen fundraisers were organized with a hurricane of support, raising thousands of dollars by those who felt helpless so many miles away. With no words communicated, people instinctively jumped into action, including setting up an explosive GoFundMe[4]. Amazing friends, Katie, Jason, and Matt put together an incredibly successful sports memorabilia auction. Jared and Devon, local restaurateurs, raised 10,000 dollars and hand delivered it to Nico and Jess in Vancouver! There were pub nights, kids' events, and more. As I recall the generosity, my eyes still fill with tears. Yet, one of the greatest gifts is knowing that no matter what happens, there is no doubt that love and good exists. If you allow it to—that is the key.

## Making Room For It All

I remember having had in-depth conversations with our family about accepting the help, opening to the grace, and not allowing any feeling but thanks being the return. So many of us have grown up feeling we are alone, that we must do everything ourselves, and if we don't, we will fall into the realm of weak and incapable. A heartfelt challenge to anyone going through a hardship, especially one that seems insurmountable. Sit for a quiet moment, open your heart, and ask… ask for help. While that may seem simple, I assure you it is not. It is one of the greatest lessons in vulnerability. Ego aside, heart contrite, body humbled, the magic is undeniable. Complete strangers, quasi acquaintances, distanced friends all become family. Their

---

[4] https://ca.gofundme.com/

motive for giving, calling, messaging? Love. Love for someone who is hurting as maybe they once hurt.

*I learned so very fast that an exquisite benefit to being human is allowing and trusting others to come through and then, whenever possible, doing the same for them.*

Interestingly, as surprising as it was to have strangers step forward sometimes, we also experienced the deafening silence from some of our close friends and family. Yet again, although confusing at first, that became a gift. As stated, life is messy, and it can sometimes cripple good motives. Fear can numb a nerve and paralyze the best intention. Childhood cancer is no joke. Even if not experienced personally, trauma can cause triggers at an alarming rate and possibly for reasons unknown. We felt this. There were absences that, in all honesty, hurt at a cerebral level—but only for a moment. I soon realized that sometimes there isn't a capacity for caring. Without discovering this revelation on purpose, I am grateful to say that it opened a deeper space inside of me for grace. It has been extended to me many, many times, and I now have the opportunity to do the same.

Human beings are made up of a tangled web of feelings, and sometimes, gathering them up and trying to make sense of them is just too much. So, they don't. Some have reached out since we've been home to apologize because they couldn't dig deep to message us. Forgiveness. Some, we never heard from again. Forgiveness.

## Nothing is Hard Anymore

Through this, as our community lifted us through the darkest moments, realizations of a new way of living started to emerge. Somewhat prophesied, I suppose as we and all the world had to find a way to navigate the besieges of COVID and what our new normal is. I felt like a pioneer. I've already taken the wagon west, searched for new land, and saw what was important and what wasn't worth my time. I'm lucky, I guess.

In 2018 I found myself at a crossroads as to what to do with my life. I have always called myself a *solution seeker* and have tried to align my secular work with my passions, and for the most part, I've done a pretty good job. However, after working for three and a half years in the not-for-profit sector, I felt a little lost as to what my next step would be. So, I did some soul-searching and heavy lifting, and I felt moved to make a difference in the arena of men's mental health. So, I started a tech company with one of my best friends, and we proceeded to take on the challenge of building a mobile app for men's health. Because…why not? By late 2019, we were headfirst and eyeball deep in research, development, contracts, building, coding, branding, moving, and shaking. I experienced the roller coaster of a new business and the death-defying drops of a start-up tech company, and I was in love. I can sink my teeth into a business like it's coated in chocolate and filled with whip cream. I live for it. But as much as I live for the adrenaline rush of building, it all came to a screeching stop when my baby got sick. Plans. Well-laid plans that go flying out the window with three words—*she has cancer.*

As we settled into the rhythm of the cancer dance, I started feeling comfortable with going back to work in any corner I could find in the hospital. Sometimes, I snuck into private rooms meant for conferencing. It's amazing what you can pull off with a laptop and air pods; people think you belong there. Other times I worked on the floor. However, all of it was secondary to my role as Glamma because that was when everything else could wait. Once again, the only reason I got away with that was my reliance on others for help and support. This theme of being vulnerable was a lesson that crashed into my hard-headed skull time and time again. And this time, it came from my angelic co-founder Shannon, who single-handedly kept our business afloat. When I look back to that time and fast forward to where we are now, I think the only appropriate word to describe it would be *divine*. How else would a brand-new company taking on a global crisis, survive a four-month absence of its CEO and still keep living? Divinity in the form of a partner, that's how.

It has been said that ideas needing to be born are given to those who will provide their best chance of survival. I remember reading that and thinking: *Wow, this idea chose poorly. How will we get through this with me only being able to give ten percent at best?* And here, here came one of the most surprising lessons that changed the trajectory of my business, deepened our partnership and quite frankly, has assured our success. Are you ready for it?

**Lesson:** Is it hard? Yes. Is it cancer? Nope. Let's go...
I cannot tell you how many times a day I repeat this. And how is this for a mind-blowing revelation? I have been playing small my whole life for fear of failure because, God forbid, something doesn't work out. So, I took only the chances that were close to being sure things. What a colossal waste of time. There is literally nothing anymore that I don't think I can't accomplish. I have witnessed the tiniest little body spring back from having a giant tumour removed. I have seen blood being drawn out of her chest while she gently tickles the nurse's arm to make her laugh. I have been privy to her being tethered to an IV pole as

three different machines administered a lethal combination of nausea medication and chemotherapy, and as soon as she was able, she threw on her shoes to run the aisles of the hospital. **NOTHING**. I repeat, **NOTHING** is harder than that. No phone call, no ask, no deal will ever come close to the bravery that this two-year-old taught me. No risk of the game of will it or won't it work? compares to the risk of will or won't she survive? There was no longer a valid excuse for me not to just go for it. To take it head-on and let it know who's boss. My beast of a granddaughter taught me more about life in four months than I ever knew before. Is it hard? Sure. Is it cancer? Nope... let's go.

**Blessing:** I am better. At everything.

# VII

## Faith and Trust

### Leaning Into My Strong Roots

February brought a rhythm to it that was both unsettling and welcomed. It was unsettling because it made me dizzy with awareness of how fast life adjusts to new *normals*. However, I welcomed the belief that without those very adjustments, we become untethered and feel like a gust could take us away, never to be seen again.

Throughout the process of Elara's illness, we became nomadic. Fun fact, years ago, when my parents travelled to Austria to meet with family members that they never had the opportunity to meet before, they found out there was gypsy in our bloodline. My mom instantly exclaimed **THAT'S WHERE CANDY**—my nickname—**COMES FROM!!** I have always been different from my family. Louder, more colourful, square-peg-round-hole different. I used to relish the stories my parents told me about how they had these three quiet kids brimming with good behaviour, and then I came screaming into existence, hellbent on disruption. Between you and me, I love and am pretty proud of that. So, to find out that I had bonafide gypsy blood in me gave me a sense of belonging and an explanation other than, *She's just different.*

While we were in Vancouver, the migrating blood given by my wayfaring ancestors certainly helped the situation. We moved eight times in four and a half months. Sometimes, we didn't even know where we would end up. Once, we sat in the parking lot of a Save On, with all our possessions crammed into the car as torrential rain crashed down around us. We slept, waiting for a bolt of inspiration to take us to our next resting place.

In the early part of our ordeal, places were easier to come by without taking a second mortgage out to finance them. Plus, remember, we thought we would only be there two weeks tops. So, as we moved further into her treatment, the city moved into spring, which meant fewer and more expensive accommodations were available.

*Unfortunately, every time we moved,*
*I watched my effervescent husband lose a little more of his soul.*
*He is not nomadic, but instead,*
*lays roots strong and deep like a dependable oak.*

It was hard to watch him struggle through that time. Not wanting to take away from what anyone else was feeling, I saw the conflict rise and fall in his chest as our time at each place came closer to the end. This is another reason I love him and another reason I felt the inherent and familiar tug of unworthiness as I battled the intrusive thought about why someone would willingly sacrifice all he had.

One of our more unique accommodations we stayed in can only be classified as a Brady Bunch house. It was a perfectly preserved mid-century split level complete with an orange kitchen and purple bathroom. I instantly fell in love. There was something incredibly comforting about being in a space that reminded me of a home I grew up in. The home was owned by a billionaire who lived overseas but managed by one of the loveliest couples with whom we became good friends. We actually stayed in their home right after moving from the Fairmont, and we loved it. Unfortunately, we could only stay a short while as they were booked. However, they had another rental, this seventies sweetheart, that was even closer to the hospital right around the corner. Perfect right? Well, yes, except it was a huge four-bedroom house that went for hundreds a night. We realized that our dwindling budget would be overrun when we multiplied that amount by the number of weeks we had left.

So, one night, I stayed up late and meditated and prayed for a sign, a miracle, anything that would prove everything would be okay. Miracles, signs, or messages don't always happen instantaneously—in my experience anyway. One usually presents when you aren't thinking of it. Or maybe even when you forgot about it. I would expect there are varying theories on this, the foremost being that faith and trust are needed, and faith only shows up when you succumb and let go. This is not the easiest task for a lover of control such as myself. However, in situations of life and death, it seems to be a prerequisite of survival. There is no control to be had. There is only hanging on with what sometimes feels like the tiniest part of your fingernails.

After moving a couple more times to some places that, for one reason or another, were disruptive and uncomfortable, we got a call. It came from our incredible friends, Kandes and Damon, who managed the aforementioned seventies house. It turns out a previous renter did some damage, and as per Air BNB rules, they were compensated monetarily. So, how did we get to stay in this completely perfect accommodation? These angels proceeded to use that compensation to offer us this house; this house, so close to the hospital, this house that meant bringing Elara home from her treatment to room to play and sleep and eat. And it was at a rate we could afford for an **EXTENDED** period of time, three weeks to be exact! This would take us to the beginning of March, which by all indications, would begin the winding down of our stay. We would potentially only have to move one more time before our trek home. Glory, glory hallelujah. This was jaw-dropping evidence of miracles, and gifts, and extreme generosity. I'll never forget that feeling, and to this day, I conjure up the memory to remind myself of how love from strangers feels. I vowed that one day I would reciprocate that level of love.

As we ride the freeways of a changing world, we must remember that there are exit signs leading us to love. A place to pull over to stop and rest, get a bite, or lay our head. I feel that sometimes, once we start on our way in life, we tend to stay on those freeways, seemingly wanting to reach our destination faster. This becomes troubling because, realistically, none of us will make it out alive, so why the rush? On that day, I witnessed friendship and companionship before there was a basis to do so. We were brought together by the love of children and family and a desire to be human. One night during our stay, this extraordinary family with their two beautiful girls came and shared an endless pan of homemade enchiladas with us. Our *sick* baby squealed with delight as her two new friends ran and chased her around the retro living room, forever changed.

## Home For a Minute

Those three weeks were the sweetest reprieve. The kids came and stayed in one of the extra rooms for a while, giving them a break from their one-room suite at the Ronald McDonald House. It also gave us the chance to be ever so present. Our youngest kids travelled over for a weekend stay, as did my mom, who I hadn't seen since my dad died. We relished the reunion of family that I didn't realize how much I needed until they crossed the door's threshold, and I wept rivers. For that time, I could sit and relax without corralling our things, ready for the next move. Hell, I even hung my clothes up in the closet for the first time in months. Small things, yes? Small things that are far too often taken for granted.

However, time ticked on, and we needed to make other arrangements soon. As much as they wanted, the owners could not extend our stay because they had long-term renters coming in. I tried to remind myself of gratitude every time I opened my computer to start searching the rental sites again and again but could feel the rise of anxiety creeping back. Regaining his mojo, Mike continuously pointed out how the universe had our back. We had just witnessed that with the magic of receiving this rental—at the exact time needed, in the exact location desired, with the exact friendship packaging it all up. Why, oh why was my gratefulness so short-sighted. I clearly needed a new prescription of understanding that things will work out no matter what. Any time I felt my anxiety climbing, all I could do was trust. How many more miracles did I have to witness before that would sink in? The truth is that we may never quite know that answer. If you suffer from anxiety as I do, the reality is that the brain releases chemicals in patterns that defy our logical self. I thankfully figured out that allowing the space for the release and subsequent retreat of these chemicals made way for my logical brain to return. I learned this through our ordeal. In the forty-plus years I have lived on this planet, I never put this sentence together until now...

*This is just a release of a chemical telling my brain
things are out of control.
But in reality, they are not.
In reality, things are fine and going to work out,
but my brain just needs a minute.*

## It Happened Again

About four days before being homeless again, I went through
the repetitious process of opening my computer to check *the
sites.* This entailed running through every rendition of AirBNB,
VRBO, Hotwire, and the likes. I checked them on the daily to
see if anything changed—nothing had. Prices were still 5000
dollars or more for a month, and sometimes, that was for just
one room in a house. Crazy. However, this day was different.
This day, I trusted myself, going back into my Rolodex of
*What did I do before that worked. Did it work?* and *Do it again,
rhetoric.* I teach this in my practice. The body has a path of least
resistance  mentality. It's how patterns form. We come across
a situation, good or bad, and the body instantly searches its
memory banks for a similarly encountered experience. It then
pushes through roll call, remembering how it handled it before,
all while asking: *When you responded this way, did you die? No?
Good, do that again.* As I said before, this can be used for both
good and bad. On the day in question, I bore down and forced
myself to use this for good. What did I do before I received
those life-altering gifts of weeks of accommodations? I asked
for them. Right, let's do that again, shall we?

So, I did. Only I didn't automatically move to *the sites.*
This time, I opened Facebook of all things. Only not to peruse
the ramblings of my quasi acquaintances but to check out its
marketplace. And there, in its glory, was a place in Vancouver

for the exact time we needed at a price we could afford. Surely, this was too good to be true? Was it a scam? Ah, there you are, you sneaky little defence system, never too far away to protect and serve—*insert eye-roll here.*

After this brief wrestling match with the negative nuance that slammed my amygdala, I wrote a brief-ish message to the owner and pressed send before I could rescind it. Intrusive thoughts notwithstanding, I went with belief and trust, closing my Mac, lying my head down, and exhaling faith. Within a few hours, I had a response. He asked if we could come to see the place the next day. Of course, we can: *What would be the best time for you to murder us? AM or PM?* As tongue-in-cheek as that seems, I wish I could say it didn't enter my head: faith and trust.

After determining the best day and time to meet, we set our google map and headed out. As we drew closer to the address, my fear turned into excitement. I guess what they say is true; it's the same nervous system response with the difference being how it's channelled. We pulled up to the coolest building on the street. If I were a starving artist in a big city, this is the building I would pray to reside in. It screamed creativity. We buzzed the intercom and waited for our guy. A young man one could only describe as having a gentle aura, opened the door. Relief immediately flooded my cortex, and I remember saying a silent thank you. We were ushered into one of four penthouse suites in the building. It had a vaulted roof, soaring floor-to-ceiling windows, a rooftop garden, and sweeping views of the city.

Pinch me. A not so brief conversation ensued. Shap was a budding start-up founder, heading to California for three months to chase his dream. He was subletting this oasis while he was gone. Although he was looking for someone for the entire three months, he soon dismissed the fact that we only needed it for one as we rambled over musings of business development, yoga, and the need to change the world. We were both smitten, and my only thought as we were leaving was: *This is the reward for holding fast and keeping faith. This is a place I would dream of living, where I could create and heal on the final leg of this journey.* Faith and trust gave me a gift.

On March 3, 2020, we packed our bags for what we believed and hoped was our final spot before going home. And what a spot it was! In anticipation of the move, we talked of walks through the city and to the ocean. Just steps outside our door were shops, markets, and more restaurants than you can shake a stick at—so much fun. We would ruminate on what we would do after leaving the hospital and where we would decompress. Sitting on the rooftop after our morning yoga, we discussed writing this book. Light began entering my eyes again, and it lifted my wings.

## The *VID* Comes a Knocking

We did those things…for about five days. And then, in what seemed like a blink of an eye, shortly after moving to our downtown oasis surrounded by hundreds of thousands of people, the globe shut down.

> *ARE YOU F\*\*\*\*ING KIDDING ME?*
> *A PANDEMIC!*
> *MY BABY IS GOING THROUGH CANCER,*
> *AND YOU GAVE ME A PANDEMIC!*

I cannot lie. I deep dived into one of the grandest scales of despair. I scoured news sites. I watched social media channels like they were church. I called my friends and family and cried. None of it changed anything. The world shut down. The restaurants around us closed. The shops boarded their windows. The streets emptied. People lined up at the local Costco day and night. I sent Mike out for food to stock up, anything to make me feel prepared in a place that wasn't mine and in a world I was unfamiliar with. Like everyone else on the planet, those first few days of the pandemic were fraught with pain and uncertainty. Suddenly, this place I so looked forward to became a prison, and everyone around me became the enemy. I grappled with and painfully concluded that, if I were to survive, I needed to change my thinking and adjust my space. I needed to rely on what had gotten me safely to this point. I needed faith and trust.

**Lesson:** Faith and trust are life rafts, but you are the only one who determines whether they get deployed. A raft is nothing if not inflated. Both require cultivation, especially in a cynical world, but they can quite literally mean the difference between life and death.

**Blessing:** My relationship with these two five-letter words is now intimate. They waited for me to show up, and gratefully, I did. They don't have a timeline; it's not too late.

# VIII

## My Dance With Change

### The Grace We Show is the Grace We Will Receive

Life gives us many opportunities to go deep. Sometimes as the heaviness swirls around us in times of stress, the chance to test the muscles we worked during the off-season is offered. The ones we develop during times of peace and quiet provide us with space for self-reflection and growth. We don't grow for the hell of it; we grow to survive. It's a natural process of life—either adapt or suffer. Although it may sound bleak, it is not. It made the survival of wars, sickness, tribulations, and pain of our ancestors permissible. We were gifted this beautiful reward of endurance with the end goal being preservation; simply put, survival.

I know that each of our experiences with COVID, the lockdown, and the shrapnel that came with it are unique. Our collective stories range in magnitude from the smallest hills to the tallest peak of the Rocky Mountains, with each person having their day of reckoning. Perhaps you've witnessed people who have flourished as they saw an *opportunity* to be introspective. From there, habits and disciplines were created that will likely be further developed as time goes on. Others went into a deep, dark cave of Netflix and Skip the Dishes. Neither is bad, and neither is better. All is survival.

Witnessing the four months we went through while

meditating on the lessons that came from it, one thing became glaringly obvious: every one of us has the right, the duty, and the obligation to live our life according to how we see fit. As a recovering people pleaser, I say this with complete aplomb. Over the course of our ordeal, we had tremendous support, with a massive community backing us. However, that doesn't mean there weren't those who felt otherwise and let us know it. Together, our family chose to share Elara's passage through cancer on social media, as well as conventional media. Watching it, you would have seen the ups of great test results and the lows of pure unadulterated fear. We found it is both liberating and terrifying to experience that depth of vulnerability. Some felt we were exploiting our granddaughter's illness, perhaps taking advantage of the generosity we received. Some even went so far as to question if she was, in fact, sick. I know this is shocking because all anyone had to do was look at her pale skin and bald head or our weary tear-stained cheeks to see the truth we were living. Debating our integrity sincerely put a strain on our family because it's hard not to take something like that personally. This scenario brings me back to how we handle things - it isn't necessarily good or bad, it just is. However, the grace we show is the grace we will receive.

## Jasmine and Aladdin Have Nothing on This *Whole New World* Deal

When COVID showed up, so did obsessive intrusive thoughts, again. While in the hospital, I went to the extreme, thinking that one of us could contract the virus and spread it to Elara. This speculation was dark and loaded with land mines that could blow me up, literally and figuratively, at any moment. So, I reached down to my roots again, and connected to the core of all that brought me here, including faith, trust… and presence. Always back to presence. Every day was a new opportunity to stay healthy and rely on all we learned to this point. The fact of the matter is our family had been in a lockdown of sorts since Christmas day. Even though we were allowed to go to stores and restaurants, we were advised and chose to see very few people. We kept her away from the busy people soup served in most metropolises. As I witnessed the chaos that started to ensue, toilet paper shortages notwithstanding, I rooted down and took each day as it came; neither good, neither bad.

As the world began adjusting to its new normal, we were slowly winding down. Each day brought a new *end*. One was an end to hospital visits for Mike and me. Only her parents were allowed in as the toll of the virus intensified. Millions around the world soon experienced their hospitals becoming hot spots of transmission and ultimately fortresses. We could no longer go in as the pack in which we travelled up to this point. So, for her last chemo, blood tests and scans, we had to wait, sometimes not so patiently, outside the hospital doors. While that may seem insignificant in the grand scheme of things, it seemed like a cruel joke to us.

For four months, we had been told about and waited for the opportunity to *ring the bell*. Should you have travelled this cancer journey or been alongside someone who moved through theirs, the bell is a pretty big deal. It signifies the end, celebrating the victory of accomplishing the monumental task you received, as well as the *all-clear*. That bell lets everyone know you did it. We even bought her a Rey from Star Wars costume because she was our Jedi who defeated the Empire.

### *Plot Twist: we didn't get to ring the bell with her.*

Life is full of disappointing moments. The times we didn't get the girl, the boy, the job, the house, the car, the shoes. How we sit in that disappointment can often determine the amount of rot that comes from it. Were we upset that we couldn't go in and ring the damn bell? Of course. But the big picture is that it didn't change the outcome. Symbolisms have a way of screwing up the true resonance of what we are trying to accomplish. We spend thousands, if not hundreds of thousands, on weddings, funerals, and births, symbolizing the act, but at the end of the day, the meaning of the celebration can never be outshone. As she got her *all-clear* that day, the truth lay in the fact that she got through a major milestone in the first act of her play. And despite a pandemic and the hospital being at full capacity, her brilliant oncologist Dr. C. and phenomenal nurse Suzanne masked up and came to celebrate at the front door.

VIP Door service…I'll take it.

## Rooftop Celebrations

I will try to explain the feeling we had as we left the hospital on her last day, but I know I won't do it justice. It was *waiting-to-go-on-a-trip-of-a-lifetime* excitement. It was *running-a-marathon-and-not-just-completing-but-competing* excitement. It was potentially over. With cancer, you don't get definitive answers at the outset. There is still trepidation at success. So, although we were ecstatic, we went to our apartment in the sky and cautiously waited until her last tests were read, evaluated, and discussed. We were days from Easter and making plans, plans to go home.

As we waited for the *all-clear*, we simultaneously watched the world close, and subsequently, humanity open. Along with the rest of the globe, we witnessed countless acts of bravery from frontline workers, health workers, and those who put their lives in danger to ensure our protection. During this time, we often brought Elara to our temporary home's rooftop to participate in the ritual embodying the symbol of our connection. We joyously celebrated as hundreds of thousands banged pots and pans, blew whistles, shot fireworks or honked horns while emerging front line workers and heroes transitioned to or from their seven-p.m. shift. Elara always squealed in glee as we screamed, yelled, whistled, cried, and laughed. Many times, we did Facebook lives, so all her supporting fans could watch her giggle. They willingly volunteered their relief in the form of typed instant messages that came faster than we could respond.

The imagery of these evening parties was not lost on me. While the greater show was for those dealing with COVID, and deservedly so, I found myself yelling a little louder, clapping a little harder, and whistling with more ferocity because, while they were busy saving humanity, they also saved my baby. What an eternal blessing. While being joined by thousands, I released gratefulness from the soul of my being into the crisp spring sky for all those who serve. Abundantly beholden.

## Living Room Dance Parties for Five

After going through anything life-changing, you soon realize the strength of character you developed and the depth of perseverance you tapped into. You suddenly find yourself being able to handle a lot of shit. The train tends to leave the tracks, while one is **WAITING** for the event to take place.

The *anticipation* can draw extended periods of joy, grief, or something in between.

**"There is no terror in the bang, only in the anticipation of it."**

**~Alfred Hitchcock**

Anticipating the *all-clear* was a long, long wait. So, as expected, the release of emotions flooded the moment we received it. At this point, that little hyphenated phrase translated into *all-clear for right now.* That is the protocol for cancer until a certain amount of time has passed. But she cleared the first hurdle. As tears flowed down our cheeks and soaked our shirts, sheer emotion cascaded to the floor. Then, seemingly out of nowhere, music started playing, and we instantly danced around the sun-filled room. Our sweetest fuzzy-head baby yipped and hollered with us as we two-stepped around the room and yelled, letting go of every single pent-up, conscious and unconscious response that lay dormant in the deep corners of our minds. Pools of dread, sadness, fear, anxiety, angst, despair, worry, panic… now lay in a puddle at our jigging feet. I highly recommend dance parties. The celebration symbolizes closure and gives your soldiered body a reason to rejoice and let go.

**Atmospheric Re-entry**

And so began the countdown. Giving ourselves the weekend to finish up any last-minute things that needed to be done, we set our sights on April 12th to make the trek home. Although we were only a mere four hours from home, we may as well have been residing on Mars for the last four months. I had disengaged from almost every other aspect of my life. I hadn't paid any attention to what could possibly be going on at home, pandemic, or no pandemic. As I packed what seemed to be the never-ending suitcases to come home, I batted thoughts back and forth of just saying screw it and leaving all my stuff by the dumpster in the back: *Do we really need to bring it home?*

Yes, we did. Our youngest kids came down with a truck, and we strategically packed the overused, over-worn, over-loved items that had cradled us through this time. I watched as, one by one, the pieces that supported my extremely minimalist world got loaded: *How did I live with such little stuff?* We spent the majority of our time in less than 500 square feet, and not only did we survive, we also didn't suffer. In my opinion, we spend so much time and money investing in stuff that overcomplicates our lives. Seeing it loaded in the truck, I realized a monumental shift in thinking...something must change at home because material things no longer mattered.

As we drove home, coming over the crest of a familiar mountain to our native bridge and lake, I felt the now very familiar sting of emotion making its way up my chest into my throat, hovering on suffocation. Never before in history have we given so much thought to emotions and how they affect us. Positive thinking is a banner that gets waved at ceremonious ventures, assuring the assailants that if they *only think good thoughts, only good thoughts come.*

> *But what we don't factor in is that ANY emotion impacts our physiology, and denying the source and rendering of those emotions can have the adverse effect we are looking for.*

In other words, toxic positivity can have more ghastly consequences than leaning into all the feels does. And so, I leaned. Hard. Sobbing as we crossed the bridge into my city of birth, I, in fact, realized everything had changed.

I changed the way I look at the buildings, old and new. I changed my response to seeing human suffering on the streets. I changed my annoyance of traffic to a curiosity of watching every twist and turn of the road with a new fascination of how I could explore it in the coming days, weeks, months. But I changed more than all that.

Walking into our home that we hadn't set foot in since Christmas Day, I realized I had indeed changed forever. I looked around at the toys still in the bathtub from the night we discovered the lump. I glanced over at our bedspread, still rumpled from when I threw my suitcase on the bed to *pack a couple of things for a couple of days*. Time had stood still within those four walls, and none of it mattered. I have never been to outer space, nor have I personally talked to anyone who has experienced such an ordeal. However, from what I have read and heard, I imagine re-entry into the atmosphere must burn up more than just the outer shell of the aircraft. It is difficult to envision how small we actually are within this vast space we call our universe when taking in the whole picture of earth from that far away. Experiencing this must truly transform the daily mundane annoyances we routinely complain about, making them seem completely frivolous and out of place.

I imagine that one's heart also goes through a similar atmospheric burn of sorts, clearing away the debris of nuanced worries, knowing that life is bigger, and indeed, far more precious than any of us give it credit for. I can visualize these things because I saw a bigger picture of our fragility for the first time in my life, being removed from the daily pressures I allowed myself to routinely succumb to. I explored entering unknown territories, witnessed terrifying possibilities, battled the elements, and overcame it all. As a family, I suppose we confronted a new frontier and won. Nothing was the same anymore. I looked around my home, which felt small and confining in the past, but now, it felt too big and unnecessary. Mike and I looked at each other and simultaneously burst into tears. They were not tears of sadness or happiness. Instead, they signified something new, coming through a baptism of fire with renewed hope.

We had the *luck* of seeing our precious little girl go to combat, battle hard, and win. Not every family gets that. Not every family we met along our journey went home with their child. We witnessed a lot of loss, and we witnessed a lot of victories. However, regardless of which way their journey went, we witnessed change. William Burroughs said: *When you stop growing, you start dying.* I never meditated on those words more effectively than I did during the time of Elara's cancer. Change isn't to be feared; it's to be revered. We learn from each trial, and from each test, we reveal more of our character and discover more insights. Some change comes from utter devastation. Still more comes from triumph and jubilation. But all transition forces growth. What we choose to do with it depends on how we want to show up in the world as a helper or a martyr.

I choose to help because, within helping, I continue to learn, to advance, to evolve. Writing this book allowed me to share my experience and hopefully provide the understanding and observation that life events unfold with us, not to us. As you read this, and if you are going through something difficult, may your lessons soften the lesions that appear, and may you find comfort in your rebirth. If you have graciously escaped a trial of monumental nature, the kind that twists and shapes life in opposite directions…then you've been blessed. My ask is that you provide grace to those who are, strength to those who do, and support to those who face unprecedented tests. Because while tomorrow can never be promised, change can be.

**Lesson:** I will never take the hours left in my life for granted. I will no longer worry about the small things that take up big space. I will never underestimate the power of prayer, collective thought, and will. I will allow time to feel and lean into understanding how this will make me a better mother, grandmother, wife, daughter, sister, friend—a human being. I will provide grace where I haven't, realization when I should, and discernment when I can't. I will never forget, but I will always move forward and try my best because…

My final

Blessing

is that

**She Changed Me**

# Testimonial

*How do I begin to describe two of the most incredible grandparents and parents I've ever met? They love fiercely and open their hearts to everyone along the way. Their love for each other is evident but witnessing the love they have for their granddaughter Elara was powerful. They embraced the journey to the awful world of cancer with such grace and dignity. Through the ups and downs, they never gave up on their little fighter. To read the perspective of both of them and read the lessons they learned along the way was so wonderful. I have had 30 years of being a paediatric nurse and witnessing these types of lessons, so it was amazing to see them in writing. To finally understand why Mike wore those ears every day makes sense now, and he wore them proudly because they meant more than just toy ears. The Chisholm family lit up the hallways of the clinic, and I thank them for letting me be a part of their journey. XO*

~ Suzanne Horn
Nurse Clinician

# About The Author

Candace is a self-described *local girl with global goals*. Having always had a penchant for leaving the world better than she found it, she continues to be on a mission to create the change she wishes to see.

From founding and running He Changed It and She Changed It, a global health tech start-up, to punctuating each day with the unbridled love for her kids and grandbaby, she embodies her emotional support quote:

### *Nevertheless, she persisted*

*She Changed Me* is Candace's first published book, but after having been nibbled by the writing bug, she knows this won't be her last. The lessons and blessings laid out in this passage are profoundly personal, and yet, universal in meaning.

Whether dealing with cancer, yourself or with a family member, a global pandemic, or heartbreak of love, Candace designed this story to nurture and help guide you. She defines human as: being, relating to, and belonging. Through the combination of her work and writing, Candace encourages everyone to experience and share opening the door to acceptance and healing—first of yourself, and then of others.

**shechangedit.com**
**hechangedit.com**

# *Acknowledgements*

Mike: Ditto.

Haha, I kid—kind of. I actually did decide to write my thank-yous AFTER my brilliant husband wrote his. And, as opposed to the book itself, I decided to read his before writing mine, mostly because his memory is something quite out of this world. He didn't disappoint in his accolades and notes of love. So, not to avoid the work, but simply because I couldn't put it any better, please know that I echo everything he wrote. That being said, I do want to personally thank a few people as well.

First, Nico and Jessica, without you, there wouldn't be an ethereal creature who has changed us all for the better. Thank you for trusting in us to be with you on this journey. Like any family, we had our ups and downs, but one thing remained constant—there is no way this baby did not feel loved every second of every day. We look forward to continued adventures with you.

Austin and Savannah, our *little kids*. Thank you for holding down the fort for what we thought was two weeks but wasn't. Dealing with our demon cat for four months is no joke :) Thank you two for coming to see us when I was missing home so badly, and Austin, for putting your video skills to work and creating a memory of Elara at the beginning of her journey that still makes me cry.

My family, I appreciate you all so much for the love.

Holly, your care packages gave me life, and Paris, your generosity will never go unappreciated. Love you all.

Bonnie and Mike, my in-laws, I bet you never expected so much excitement when your son got married, hey? LOL. Thank you for your constant support and for being an incredible *Gigi* and *Grumps* to our Elara bear. We love you.

FRIENDS!!! Oh my gosh. Thank you to so many friends who stepped up and literally called, texted, gifted, sent love and everything in between. I mention many in the book, but again, the list is long, and Mike did an extraordinary job making sure to include as many as possible. Added to that list are:

Alexandra, Katherine, and Crystal for putting together the most incredible kids' event as a fundraiser. Despite super inclement weather and a pandemic, you pulled it off, and your generosity was outstanding;

Cayman and Lucas for the GoFundMe, and for coming to put a smile on our faces—diverting travel and all;

Rhonda Norman, for putting together a fundraiser at her pub so quickly;

Jonxy and Katia, thank you for your late-night chats that kept me sane;

Lisa, that Instagram live we did on the rooftop had me feeling all the feels, and just seeing your face made it better;
Alex, Cindy, and all Mike's—and now my—cousins, Ian, Pansy, and Snow, your care package and treat of dinner were so needed and came at the perfect time!

I know I am forgetting some, but please, please know that it is simply my brain, not my heart. Every single one of you who contacted us and sent us your energy will forever be woven into our journey's fabric.

The TOP GUN team of Children's Hospital and RMH: Dr. B., Dr. C., Suzanne, Holly, and every single member we came in contact with in each facility, I love you. So very, very, much. You are pure magic, and there is no way on this planet that we would be where we are without you. Fun fact…I often say that I don't get intimidated often anymore—I mean, I'm 50. But when I met Dr. C. for the first time, in all her six-foot glory, I swear I could hear Kenny Loggins playing *Danger Zone*. She embodied the best of the best. There was never a better time in my life for my reverence. You didn't disappoint. We had the dream team, and we will never ever forget that.

Diana, our editor, mentor, coach, but most importantly, friend, you encouraged and coaxed every word out onto these pages, and the loving way in which you did that made this not only a great experience but one I would repeat. That's saying something. Not always after birthing a *baby* like this book is, does one want to turn around and do it again. Thank you for the guidance. It proved to be worth its weight in gold, and I would recommend you to every single budding writer I know.

My Dad, ahhhhhh, what to say here without crying as I type. Losing you one month before going straight into Elara's cancer was almost more than I could bear. I didn't know how I would or could do it. But then, all the strength you taught me flooded my system and made me stronger than I thought humanly possible. And in one fell swoop, I saw how your dedication to family is all that ever really mattered. Your bond with Nico moulded him into a father that legends are made of. Thank you for your years of service, Dad. I miss you more than words can say, but I know I'm going to be okay. I love you from the basement to the sky.

Mike, we have this awesome mutual admiration society going on between us. You incessantly thank me for giving you a family, and I incessantly thank you for enveloping my family. At the end of it all, what is true is that we are a family that was meant to be. I could never have asked for a more dedicated Pa to Elara. Your love for her transcends earthly bonds, and I know you know that. Writing this book with you was challenging, emotional, but ultimately, one of the most rewarding things I have done. I never doubted our connection but taking it to this cerebral level was an exercise that surprised me a little. I love that we waited to read each other's book until the end, and the payoff was seeing how it all came together. It provides reassurance that we are soul mates and meant to tackle everything this world has to offer. I love you with my heart and soul.

And finally, Elara, my boo. I hope when you are old enough to read this book, you will feel the love that we all have for you and each other. There is no valid reason for you to have gone through cancer my love, but there were blessings and lessons that your ordeal inspired for lifetimes to come, and I know when you read this, you will see that. You are powerful, strong, smart, and beautiful. You see the world for what it is, your opportunity. You have the opportunity to teach by example and to love by default. To be picked as your Mimi is a gift I will never take for granted. Thank you for giving me the title and for teaching me its true meaning. I love you from the basement to the sky.

Candace Chisholm
September 2021

After her surgery, popsicles became their own food group
bringing much needed relief to her warrior body.
Here, Elara and her Mimi are sharing in the delight.

We often referred to Elara as a Jedi,
defeating the awful Empire.
She often came up on our rooftop patio to honour the
health care workers, wearing her Jedi gear.
Forever our Rae (Rey)!

Just as she started losing her hair,
Elara started gaining the insight of the journey ahead of her.
In doing so, she gained empathy and
that showed in helping all her babies.
This doll would later be used to help her understand
upcoming procedures
she would be going through.

Three months after returning from home,
we settled back into the routine of our weekly visits.
We loved her pixie hair here.
We would never have cut her locks were it
not for losing her hair,
so to see her rocking this style was incredible.

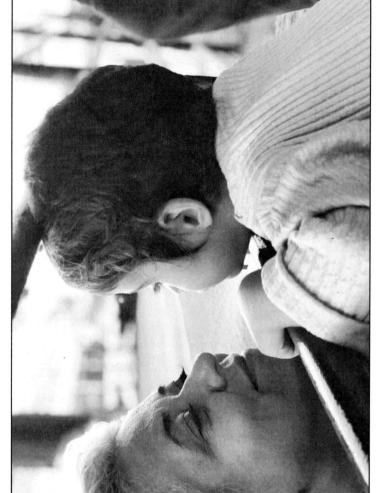

Best Friends